Economic Thought
Volume 3, Issue 1, 2014

Table of Contents

In line with the objectives of the World Economics Association, this journal seeks to support and advance interdisciplinary research that investigates the potential links between economics and other disciplines as well as contributions that challenge the divide between normative and positive approaches. Contributions from outside the mainstream debates in the history and philosophy of economics are also encouraged. In particular, the journal seeks to promote research that draws on a broad range of cultural and intellectual traditions.

Economic Thought accepts article submissions from scholars working in: the history of economic thought; economic history; methodology of economics; and philosophy of economics - with an emphasis on original and path-breaking research.

Website http://et.worldeconomicsassociation.org/
Contact eteditor@worldeconomicsassociation.org

Managing editor
Kyla Rushman

Co-editors
Sheila C. Dow, UK, University of Stirling
John Latsis, UK, University of Reading
Alejandro Nadal, Mexico, El Colegio de Mexico
Annalisa Rosselli, Italy, University of Rome Tor Vergata

Editorial board
Richard Arena, France, University of Nice-Sophia Antipolis
Robert U. Ayres, France, INSEAD
Daniel W. Bromley, USA, University of Wisconsin at Madison
Bruce Caldwell, USA, Duke University
Victoria Chick, UK, University of London
David C. Colander, USA, Middlebury College
John B. Davis, Netherlands, Universiteit van Amsterdam
Jean-Pierre Dupuy, France, École Polytechnique and Stanford University
Donald Gillies, UK, University of London
Tony Lawson, UK, University of Cambridge
Maria Cristina Marcuzzo, Italy, La Sapienza, Università di Roma
Stephen Marglin, USA, Harvard University
Manfred Max-Neef, Chile, Universidad Austral de Chile
Deirdre McCloskey, USA, University of Illinois at Chicago
Erik S Reinert, Norway, The Other Canon
Alessandro Roncaglia, Italy, La Sapienza, Università di Roma
Irene van Staveren, Netherlands, Erasmus University

ISSN 2055-6314 (print)
ISSN 2049-3509 (online)
ISBN 978-1-84890-150-6

Published by College Publications on behalf of the World Economics Association
Sister WEA open-access journals: *World Economic Review* and *Real-World Economics Review*

College Publications
Scientific Director: Dov Gabbay
Managing Director: Jane Spurr

http://www.collegepublications.co.uk

Original cover design WEA.
Printed by Lightning Source, Milton Keynes, UK

_____

Should the History of Economic Thought be Included in Undergraduate Curricula?

Alessandro Roncaglia[1], Department of Statistical Sciences, Sapienza University of Rome, Italy
alessandro.roncaglia@uniroma1.it

Abstract

Mainstream views concerning the uselessness or usefulness of HET are illustrated. These rely on a hidden assumption: a 'cumulative view' according to which the provisional point of arrival of contemporary economics incorporates all previous contributions in an improved way. Critiques of positivism led philosophy of science to recognise the existence of different approaches – in economics, as in other sciences. Conceptualisation, recognised by Schumpeter as the first stage in economic theorising, is the stage in which the different visions of the world underlying the different approaches, take shape – and are better recognised. In this, HET plays an essential role. As an illustration, the differences between the classical and marginalist conceptualisations of the economy are illustrated. Thus HET is essential in both undergraduate and graduate economic curricula, as a decisive help towards a better understanding and evaluation of formalised theories/models in the first case, and as an education to the philological method of research, essential in the first stage of theorising, in the case of graduate curricula.

Keywords: history of economic analysis, undergraduate curricula, graduate curricula, heterodox approaches, stages of economic theorising

1. The Mainstream View

'Economic theory [...] finds no necessity for including its history as a part of professional training.' In the decades since Gordon (1965, p. 126) stated this view, it has remained a mainstream tenet. It was already a mainstream tenet thirty years earlier, in the 1930s, when economists belonging to the then dominant Marshallian tradition such as John Hicks and Dennis Robertson argued that there was no point in wasting time reading the classical economists.[2] (Later, after the Sraffian Revolution and in opposition to it, Hicks

---

[1] For earlier presentations of my views, cf. Roncaglia, (1996, 2005), on which I have drawn in parts of the present paper.
[2] Letter by Robertson to Keynes, 3 February 1935, in Keynes (1973, vol. 13, p. 504); letter by Hicks, 9 April 1937, in Keynes (1973, vol. 14, p. 81).

1

began to refer to classical economists in his writings, but some erroneous references appear to confirm his earlier, more distant attitude).[3]

The declining role of the history of economic thought in undergraduate and graduate curricula has been signaled, and discussed, in a stream of papers.[4] In all likelihood, this trend has both cultural and political reasons. Tentatively – the subject would deserve specific in-depth analysis – we might suggest two distinct but possibly interacting aspects. On the one hand, we have the axiomatisation of economics: a method which hypostatises the assumptions, which are adopted for logical reasons and, once adopted, no longer require discussion of their historical roots. On the other hand, we have had the repercussions of the confrontation between Communist and Western systems – a heated confrontation, notwithstanding the Cold War label –, with a widespread (and, as a matter of fact, largely erroneous) identification of Classical with Marxian economics, where HET was perceived as the Trojan horse to infiltrate Western culture with anti-capitalist ideas.[5]

According to Gordon, history of economic thought is not useless since it can help students in gradually scaling the heights of economic theory,[6] but it remains a detour in comparison with direct perusal of contemporary economic theory. From this point of view, we may add, HET's pedagogical usefulness is reduced whenever there is discontinuity in the development of the analytical toolbox with no change in the underlying worldview, as in fact was the case after the Second World War with the publication of Samuelson's *Foundations* (1947).

Of course, this does not mean that specialists should not be allowed to devote themselves to it: as with other cultural ventures, 'we study history because it is there'

---

[3] For instance, in the first edition of *A theory of Economic History*, Hicks (1969, p. 168) erroneously stated that Ricardo had never made use of numerical examples in his *Principles*. On the revival of the history of economic thought in the wake of the Sraffian Revolution in the 1970s, cf. Marcuzzo and Rosselli (2002).

[4] Cf. in particular the papers collected in Weintraub (ed.) (2002). More recently, Caldwell (2013, p. 754) optimistically pointed to 'some recent hopeful signs of change' which however appear limited to HOPE's stronghold, Duke University.

[5] The identification of HET with heterodox economics has been lamented by, for instance, Weintraub (2002, p.6): 'if most economists understand the history of economics as an attack on mainstream economics, they will be hostile to the subdiscipline and its claims on common resources of faculty positions and students' time.' I agree in principle that such an identification is wrong: each point of view, within economics, as in any other social science, has a right, and indeed has the need, to reflect on its own roots and on the differences with other viewpoints; moreover, such research helps open confrontation between opposing viewpoints. Whatever their viewpoint may be, historians of thought should share the common philological requirements of fidelity to the text to be interpreted and attention to the context, and this should help in the inter-viewpont debate (as an example, I always enjoyed – and learned from – my discussions with Samuel Hollander). However, Weintraub makes a different point, concerning the (fundamentalist, Taliban-like) attitude of the majority of mainstream economists towards the heterodox minority, and in this respect very little can be said, apart from the fact that such an attitude should be rejected by any liberal mind, whatever the point of view adopted in economic research.

[6] A similar position is held by Blaug (2001, p. 156): 'I never understood the calculus I learned at school until I read accounts of the Newton-Leibnitz disputes about "the fundamental theorem of the calculus"'. Such experiences, however, are by no means common among students of mathematics.

(Gordon, ibid). And there is a subtle justification for inserting it in graduate economic curricula (a justification now apparently overlooked, since HET rarely gets a look in even there), which we may derive from one of the leading mainstream scholars in the field: Jacob Viner.

According to Viner, although theoretical research comes uppermost, HET may contribute to the formation of researchers. As Viner (1991, p. 385 and 390) says, 'the pursuit of broad and exact knowledge of the history of the working of the human mind as revealed in written records', namely 'scholarship', implies 'a commitment to the pursuit of knowledge and understanding': 'once the taste for it has been aroused, it gives a sense of largeness even to one's small quests, and a sense of fullness even to the small answers [...] a sense which can never in any other way be attained'. In this sense, HET is important for the education of researchers, even if it is not necessary for their training. To the many who are not willing to recognise this, Viner, with his aristocratic bent, might have answered by paraphrasing John Stuart Mill (1863, p. 281): 'It is better to be a human being dissatisfied than a pig satisfied, better to be Socrates dissatisfied than a fool satisfied. And if the fool, or the pig, are of a different opinion, it is because they only know their own side of the question'.

Along much the same lines as Viner, namely considering HET as an activity inferior to theorising, useful but not strictly required for the training of economists, we find the other leading 20th century historian of economic thought, Joseph Schumpeter. According to Schumpeter, studying economists of the past is pedagogically helpful, may prompt new ideas and affords useful material on the methods of scientific research in economics. 'We stand to profit from visits to the lumber room provided we do not stay there too long' (Schumpeter 1954, p. 4, where the qualification sounds self-ironical, considering the amount of time Schumpeter himself spent in 'the lumber room'). In other words, studying previous economists' accomplishments should not take too much of the contemporary economist's time out of theoretical and applied research. HET may nevertheless be useful, for among other things a reason similar to the one given by Viner: it 'will prevent a sense of *lacking direction and meaning* from spreading among the students' (Schumpeter, 1954, p. 4; italics in the original).

In other words, even in the context of a single paradigm, HET can help in understanding economic theories by filling out the social, political and cultural context of their origins and their diffusion, such as what problems they aim at solving or which ideas they are meant to support or to oppose.

2. The Hidden Assumption of the Mainstream View

Schumpeter implicitly pointed to other reasons, which we shall consider below, for attributing HET with an important role in economists' basic training; however, as we shall see, such reasons acquire vital significance only when a common attitude prevailing among mainstream economists is rejected. Within the mainstream approach, explicitly or – more often – implicitly (and – be it noted – not necessarily), a sort of positivist attitude dominates: economic knowledge grows over time, through accumulation of new theories and new empirical knowledge; the personalities of the economists, their ethical values or their basic vision of the world (their *Weltanschauung*) are external to the field of economic science and should, rather, be considered as belonging to the field of cultural history, together with the history of mathematics or physics.

As a matter of fact, viewing HET as belonging to the general field of the history of culture (or the history of sciences) rather than the broad field of economics is an attitude taken by some contemporary historians of economic thought.[7] This viewpoint was taken to its extreme consequences in the – luckily unsuccessful – attempts to remove HET from economic research classifications, first in Australia (by the Australian Bureau of Statistics in 2007) and then in the European Union (by the European Research Council in 2011).[8] My view is that HET belongs to both fields: a good practitioner of HET should be knowledgeable both in economic theory and in the history of culture.[9] Since the present paper is concerned with the role of HET in economic curricula, it is quite natural for the relationship between HET and economic theory to dominate the argument. As for the partition of academic careers, an opening to HET should be left in both fields, depending on the individual researcher's specialised contributions, as is the case in many other bridge disciplines.

Underlying the mainstream view on the limited usefulness of HET is a clear – though never explicitly stated – assumption, namely that there is but one correct approach to economics. We may label this a 'cumulative view': economics does change over time, but with steady progress in the understanding of economic reality, piling up new theories and new facts. As mentioned above, the toolbox of the economic theorist may change (for instance, from Marshallian U-shaped cost curves to axiomatic Arrow-Debreu general equilibrium theory), but the underlying pillar – in short, the notion of market equilibrium between supply and demand – remains the same. From this viewpoint, the provisional point of arrival of contemporary economics incorporates all previous contributions in an improved way.

---

[7] Cf. for instance Schabas (1992).
[8] The story is told by Kates (2013).
[9] On this point cf. also Marcuzzo (2008).

The 'cumulative view' has, as its methodological (but often implicit and, occasionally, unconscious) background, a positivist view of science: economic theories based on deduction from first principles (scarcity of resources, agents' preferences, demand and supply equilibrium) are either logically consistent and hence true given the premises, or logically contradictory and hence false; factual statements are once again either empirically confirmed or contradicted; science progresses as theories and knowledge of facts cumulate.

This viewpoint has been supported by mainstream historians of economic thought (from Jacob Hollander, 1904, 1910, to Samuel Hollander, 1973, 1979) through an interpretation of the classical economists that sees them following in the line of the supply-and-demand-equilibrium view, and so as perceptive but defective precursors of later views. This explains the importance of Piero Sraffa's (1951) reinterpretation of Ricardo (and with him of the whole Classical economists' approach) as embedded in a different paradigm, which can be succinctly expressed as the 'picture of the system of production and consumption as a circular process' (Sraffa, 1960, p. 93). In fact, in the 1960s and 1970s the debate between the contending paradigms proceeded along two parallel paths: the 'Cambridge controversies' in the theory of capital and distribution (as illustrated, for example. in Harcourt, 1972) and debates in the history of economic thought concerning, for instance, the role of supply and demand in the Classical (Smith's or Ricardo's in particular) theory of value and distribution.

3. The Role of HET when the Existence of Different Approaches to Economics is Recognised

As soon as we recognise the existence of different (and contending) paradigms,[10] the history of economic thought acquires a new, much more relevant, role. This is where Schumpeter's distinction between different stages in economic theorising is relevant.

In the first pages of his *History of Economic Analysis*, Schumpeter (1954, pp. 41-42) makes his well-known distinction between various stages in economic research: i) the 'pre-analytic cognitive act' or 'vision', meaning by this a vague vision of the issue to be considered and some tentative hypotheses as to the direction of research; ii) conceptualisation, namely 'to verbalise the vision or to conceptualise it in such a way that its elements take their places, with names attached to them that facilitate recognition and manipulation, in a more or less orderly schema or picture'; iii) model building and, finally,

---

[10] It is beyond the scope of this paper to discuss the critiques of positivism and the alternative methodological views (Kuhn, Popper, Lakatos, McCloskey and so on). For a very concise survey of some of these views from the point of view of the history of economic thought cf. Roncaglia (2005, chapter 1).

iv) the application of such models to the interpretation of economic reality. What matters to us here is the second stage, quite often overlooked, although Schumpeter himself attributes great importance to it.

Conceptualisation, in fact, becomes an essential aspect of the economist's work when the vision that the researcher is trying to develop differs from the visions adopted/developed by other theoreticians. It is in this stage of work that the theoretician can clarify the distinct character of her/his own representation of the world: not only the relative importance attributed to different aspects of the real world, but also and especially the perspective from which each aspect is viewed. Conceptualisation is a complex activity where, for instance, the requirement of consistency (which of course still holds) has a different, broader meaning as compared with the formal coherence required of mathematically-framed theories; in any case, conceptualisation represents the (explicit or implicit) foundation for clarifying the connection between such mathematically-framed theories and the real world. For example, a formal model of functional income distribution relies on a class representation of society; analysis of financial managers' incentives relies on the conceptualisation of a managerial (large corporations) economy rather than an economy based on small competitive firms.

It is not unusual for mainstream theoreticians to overlook the role of this stage in economic research. This is clearly due to the fact that the underlying vision of the economy is common to all of them (albeit with different nuances) and is considered the only possible one. Supply and demand reasoning reigns supreme; differences between streams of mainstream economics are a matter of the framework to which supply and demand analysis is applied, as for instance when introducing market forms other than perfect competition, imperfect and asymmetric information, and the like. Thus, it is only these latter aspects that are considered when illustrating the conceptual foundations for the activity of model-building.

On the other hand, there are profound differences in the visions of the economy underlying Classical, Keynesian and neoclassical-marginalist economics. In order to understand them, recourse to the history of economic thought is necessary: it is only when seeking through HET a direct understanding of the visions of the world of a Smith, a Ricardo, a Keynes, a Jevons or a Walras that we can perceive these differences, and the true content of the different concepts referred to in formal analyses of the economy.

Let me make myself clear. All this does not mean that HET is only useful from a non-mainstream point of view. A better understanding of the meaning of the concepts utilised in economic theorising is essential whatever the researcher's own preferred approach. It is also essential – but this is a different, additional element – for serious debate between contending approaches.[11] HET does not belong to heterodox economics: it belongs to each and every approach; it is useful, nay necessary, for economists of all persuasions. Confrontation with alternative viewpoints is in fact essential to mainstream economists for a better understanding of their own conceptual foundations.

The reason why HET appears to be more strongly connected to heterodox economics is precisely that these are minority approaches, so that confrontation is vital for them, as a means to rise in the general opinion of the economic profession, while HET is vital for this confrontation, given its role, discussed above, in clarifying the different world-view adopted by mainstream economics as well as by each group of heterodox economists. Serious debate between contending approaches should be the salt of serious research activity: the majority rule should not be adopted as a criterion to condemn dissenting views (as John Stuart Mill taught us for the political field at large). From a slightly different context, let me recall Kula's (1958, p. 234) beautiful eulogy of history: 'To understand the others: this is the historian's aim. It is not easy to have a more difficult task. It is difficult to have a more interesting one.'

4. An Illustration: Classical and Marginalist Conceptualisations of the Economy[12]

Let us briefly consider, by way of illustration, the main differences between the classical and the marginalist/neoclassical conceptualisations of the economy.

The classical economists saw the economy as first and foremost characterised by the division of labour. There is not only separation of tasks within each production process, but also specialisation of the different productive units turning out different (bundles of) commodities. Thus, at the end of each productive process, each productive unit (and each sector or, in other words, each set of productive units utilising similar production processes and producing similar commodities) needs to recover its means of production in exchange for at least part of its products. This gives rise to a web of

---

[11] Confrontation between contending approaches is useful for the scientific community at all levels, from the international community at large down to the individual university department level. So much can be maintained on three counts: as a stimulus to demonstrate through research that the viewpoint adopted amounts to a progressive scientific research programme; as a drive to greater clarity in presenting research results; and as a source of criticism essential to a conjecture-confutation scientific process. Departments in which different approaches coexist are livelier than departments where one single faith reigns supreme; this liveliness attracts bright students and constitutes a basic element in their formation as researchers. Of course, it calls for strong moral sentiments and scientific openness on the side of researchers.

[12] This outline presentation of the differences between contending approaches (for which I have drawn on Roncaglia, 2010) ignores important differences internal to each approach. We also leave aside a basic notion brought to the fore by the Keynesian approach, namely the notion of uncertainty (on the differences between the Keynesian and the Knightian notion of uncertainty, cf. Roncaglia (2009); it is this latter notion which has been embodied in the mainstream conceptual framework). For fuller illustration of the different views, cf. Roncaglia (2005).

exchanges which are necessary for the economy to subsist. Indeed, analysis of the conditions necessary for the vitality and sound functioning of a market economy based on the division of labour is the main object of the classical approach. Thus, according to the classical economists, in a market economy the exchange ratio between commodities must be such as to allow each sector to recover physical production costs and obtain profits constituting sufficient incentive to continue activity. Taking into account the dominant technology and a uniform profit rate – corresponding to the assumption of free competition, or in other words the absence of obstacles to capital movements from one sector to another – the classical economists set out to determine production prices: those prices, that is, which are compatible with regular continuation of economic activity. Within their approach, income distribution between profits and wages is not univocally determined by technical givens, and is commonly treated as an open (economic, but also socio-political) issue.

On the other hand, according to the marginalist/neoclassical approach, economic agents have at their disposal given amounts of scarce resources (or original endowments); these are then utilised to satisfy their needs and desires (directly, through exchange and consumption, and indirectly, through production processes in which productive resources are transformed into consumption goods and services). Indeed, analysis of the conditions under which resources are optimally allocated to the satisfaction of human needs and desires is the main object of the marginalist approach. The market here is a point in time and space where demand and supply meet: its archetype is the market fair, and in more recent times the stock exchange or, more precisely, the old-fashioned continental exchanges, based on call markets, even more than the continuous dealing Anglo-Saxon exchanges which constitute the rule in contemporary economies. (In the classical approach, as pointed out above, the market is a web of commodity flows, recurring period after period, which link up all sectors of the economy.) As an implication of this viewpoint, within the marginalist approach the notion of prices refers to indicators of the relative scarcity of goods and services available at each given moment in time to satisfy the needs and desires of economic agents. This implies assuming the relative intensity of needs and desires as given data in addressing the problem. In the classical approach, on the other hand, prices are indicators of relative difficulty of production;[13] the problem here is how to express in terms of value – in terms of a single magnitude, that is – all the different physical costs while at the same time respecting the distributive rules of a capitalist economy; consumption choices are analysed, rather, by reference to (social) habits evolving over time. Similar differences

---

[13] 'Relative' here refers to comparison between the different production processes; in marginalist analysis, instead, 'relative' refers to demand-supply comparison which, in a general equilibrium approach, concerns simultaneously all the goods and services in the economy.

can be illustrated for the notions of social classes and the analysis of income distribution, the notion of competition and the analysis of market forms, and so on.

5. The Role of HET in Undergraduate and Graduate Curricula

Let us conclude by summarising the implications the arguments illustrated above hold for the role of HET in undergraduate and graduate curricula.

In the first case, systematic illustration of the history of our discipline is a way to present undergraduate students with the different approaches which have existed over time, often simultaneously, and their rise and fall (which, by the way, ought to appeal to mainstream economists, who should find a reason for pride in being not the only ones around but – *pro tempore* at least – those emerging as winners from a centuries-long debate).

An execrable practice in drawing up undergraduate curricula is to include only the study of the mainstream approach in its various components. The customary excuse for this is that presenting a single truth and avoiding controversy simplifies life for the students – with, once again, the covert assumption that there is only one single 'true' approach in economics. This authoritarian attitude implies that eighteen year olds may have the right to vote in political elections but still remain so simple-minded as to get confused when confronted with a simple fact of life, namely that there are different and often conflicting viewpoints on all aspects of life, including how a market economy works. On the contrary, and even if students were unable to make up their own minds about contending economic approaches – provisionally, of course, and keeping an open mind, as we all should do – it is of the utmost importance that they be educated to take pluralism in their stride, in economics as in any other subject matter.

Thus, in undergraduate education, HET has a crucial democratic role, confronting students with the idea that there are different approaches to economics, and providing them with some notion of the conceptual foundations of such approaches: the background they emerged from and their evolution in response both to theoretical debate and to historical events. This helps towards a better understanding and evaluation of formalised theories/models, thus constituting a prerequisite for serious study of economic theory.

In the case of graduate curricula, assuming that they are designed to prepare economists for a research career, and assuming that the existence of different approaches is an already acquired component of undergraduate education, HET has a twin formative role. First, HET educates to evaluating the content of concepts and, in connection with the study of economic history (another under-represented but necessary component of economic curricula), the shift such content undergoes over time, partly in response to theoretical developments and partly in response to changes in economic realities, or in other words to history; hence, acquisition of the rhetorical method of confrontation. Second, HET educates to a method – the philological method of faithfulness to text and context – which is different from those exercised in theorising or in applied research and which is most useful in understanding the world confronting us, where culture and ideas are such an important component of the economic environment.[14] The philological method is also important for its formative character in the ethics of research: attention to details and openness to confrontation with different points of view, absence of definitive truths but consciousness of degrees of superior or inferior quality in the analysis.

The declining role if not the absence of HET from undergraduate and graduate curricula is not so much a problem for the confraternity of HET practitioners. The main loss here is in scope for the employment of our students, while an already established practitioner of this discipline can move to the fields of history of culture, or history of science. It is above all a problem for the economics discipline at large. In fact economics, a-historically interpreted as model building and applied analysis based on econometric exercises, is losing ground to business schools, faculties of political and social sciences and, above all, to sociology – which, a century ago, was a sub-discipline internal to economics itself. Economics without HET is a body without soul.

Acknowledgements

Thanks are due to Donald Gillies, Grazia Ietto, Cristina Marcuzzo and Annalisa Rosselli for reading and commenting on a previous draft. Thanks are also due to Andres Bedoya and especially to Constantinos Repapis and Nicholas Theocarakis for their contributions in the Open Peer Discussion forum on this paper, which has accordingly been substantially revised.

References

Blaug, M. (2001) 'No history of ideas, please, we're economists', *Journal of Economic Perspectives*, 15, pp. 145-64.

Caldwell, B. (2013) 'Of positivism and the history of economic thought', *Southern Economic Journal*, 79, pp. 753-67.

---

[14] This is, from a somewhat different viewpoint, the aspect stressed by Viner and discussed above.

Gordon, D. (1965) 'The role of the history of economic thought in the understanding of modern economic theory', *American Economic Review*, 55, pp. 119-27.

Harcourt, G.C. (1972) *Some Cambridge controversies in the theory of capital* (Cambridge: Cambridge University Press).

Hicks, J. (1969) *A theory of economic history* (Oxford: Oxford University Press).

Hollander, J. (1904) 'The development of Ricardo's theory of value', *Quarterly Journal of Economics*, 18, pp. 455-91.

Hollander, J. (1910) *David Ricardo - A centenary estimate* (Baltimore; repr. New York: McKelley, 1968).

Hollander, S. (1973) *The economics of Adam Smith* (Toronto: University of Toronto Press).

Hollander, S. (1979) *The economics of David Ricardo* (Toronto: University of Toronto Press).

Keynes, J.M. (1973) *The General Theory and after*, in *Collected writings*, vols. 13 (*Part I: preparation*) and 14 (*Part II: defense and development*), ed. by D. Moggridge (London: Macmillan).

Kates, S. (2013) *Defending the history of economic thought* (Cheltenham: Edward Elgar).

Kula, W. [1958]. *Riflessioni sulla storia*. Venezia: Marsilio, 1990 (English translation, *The problems and methods of economic history*, (Aldershot: Ashgate) 2001).

Marcuzzo, M. C. (2008) 'Is history of economic thought a "serious" subject?', *Erasmus Journal for Philosophy and Economics*, 1, pp. 107-23.

Marcuzzo, M. C. and Rosselli, A. (2002) 'Economics as history of economics: the Italian case in retrospect', in Weintraub (ed.), pp. 98-109.

Mill, J.S.(1863/1987) *Utilitarianism*, reprinted in Mill J.S. and Bentham, J., *Utilitarianism and other essays*, ed. by A. Ryan (London: Penguin Books).

Roncaglia, A. (1996) 'Why should economists study the history of economic thought?', *European Journal of the History of Economic Thought*, 3, pp. 296-309.

Roncaglia, A. (2005) *The wealth of ideas* (Cambridge: Cambridge University Press).

Roncaglia, A. (2009) 'Keynes and probability: an assessment', *European Journal of the History of Economic Thought*, 16, pp. 489-510.

Roncaglia, A. (2010) 'The origins of social inequality: beavers for women, deer for men', in A. Birolo, D. Foley, H. Kurz, B. Schefold, I. Steedman (eds), *Production, distribution* and trade: alternative perspectives. Essays in honour of Sergio Parrinello (London: Routledge), pp. 289-303.

Samuelson, P.A. (1947) Foundations of economic analysis. (Cambridge MA: Harvard University Press).

Schabas, M. (1992) 'Breaking away: history of economics as history of science', History of Political Economy, 24, pp. 187-203.

Schumpeter, J. (1954) History of economic analysis, ed. by E. Boody Schumpeter (New York: Oxford University Press).

Sraffa, P. (1951) 'Introduction', in Ricardo D., Works and correspondence, 10 vols., ed. by P. Sraffa, Cambridge: Cambridge University Press, 1951-55, vol. I, pp. xiii-lxii.

Sraffa, P. (1960) Production of commodities by means of commodities (Cambridge: Cambridge University Press).

Viner, J. (1991) Essays on the intellectual history of economics, ed. by D.A. Irwin (Princeton: Princeton University Press).

Weintraub, R. (ed.) (2002) The future of the history of economics. Annual Supplement, History of Political Economy, 34.

Weintraub, R. (2002) 'Will economics ever have a past again?', in Weintraub (ed.), pp. 1-14.

SUGGESTED CITATION:

Roncaglia, A. (2014) 'Should the History of Economic Thought be Included in Undergraduate Curricula?'. Economic Thought, 3.1, pp. 1-12.
http://www.worldeconomicsassociation.org/files/journals/economicthought/WEA-ET-3-1-Roncaglia.pdf

A commentary on Alessandro Roncaglia's paper: 'Should the History of Economic Thought be Included in Undergraduate Curricula?'

Nicholas J. Theocarakis[15], Department of Economics, Faculty of Economics and Politics, National and Kapodistrian University of Athens, Greece, ntheocar@econ.uoa.gr

Keywords: history of economic analysis, undergraduate curricula, graduate curricula, heterodox approaches, stages of economic theorising

In Plato's dialogue *Protagoras,* Socrates argues that because virtue cannot be taught, matters involving virtue can be addressed by all citizens. Similarly, because matters professional can be taught, they can and are addressed with authority only by their respective specialists:

> I say, in common with the rest of the Greeks, that the Athenians are wise. Now I observe, when we are collected for the Assembly, and the city has to deal with an affair of building, we send for builders to advise us on what is proposed to be built; and when it is a case of laying down a ship, we send for shipwrights; and so in all other matters which are considered learnable and teachable: but if anyone else, whom the people do not regard as a craftsman, attempts to advise them, no matter how handsome and wealthy and well-born he may be, not one of these things induces them to accept him; they merely laugh him to scorn and shout him down, until either the speaker retires from his attempt, overborne by the clamour, or the tipstaves pull him from his place or turn him out altogether by order of the chair. Such is their procedure in matters which they consider professional. But when they have to deliberate on something connected with the administration of the State, the man who rises to advise them on this may equally well be a smith, a shoemaker, a merchant, a sea-captain, a rich man, a poor man, of good family or of none, and nobody thinks of casting in his teeth, as one would in the former case, that his attempt to give advice is justified by no instruction obtained in any quarter, no guidance of any master; and obviously it is because they hold that here the thing cannot be taught. [Pl. *Prt.* 319b-d]

---

[15] Associate Professor of Political Economy and History of Economic Thought, Director of the Section of Political Economy.

In today's ideological world, however, the tipstaves are out, with a twist: they escort out those who are not deemed worthy to speak with authority on matters of state policy or political economy. However, no blunt force trauma is visible on those who persist. Expulsion is achieved in subtler ways. Take the history of economic thought (HET) as an example: Professors who retire see their chairs being reassigned to more 'scientific' fields of research within economics. More and more universities, especially those with the highest ranking scores in the Anglo-Saxon academic world, purge HET courses from their curricula altogether. Graduate courses in HET in 'top' USA universities – with the notable exception of Duke – are well-nigh absent (Gayer 2002; Weintraub 2002, 2007). Associations of Business Schools and Business Deans' Councils downgrade top-notch journals in HET blocking the hierarchical promotion of the 'harmless drudge that busies himself in tracing the original, and detailing the signification of' economic concepts (Samuel Johnson 1755). HET researchers and teachers feel as if they are working in bishoprics *in partibus infidelium*, gentlewomen in reduced circumstances. In fact, the very creation of HET as a separate discipline with its own societies and periodicals, which started in the late 1960s, was the result of a gradual refusal of major academic journals to publish work in HET (Weintraub 2007, pp. 273-4, Goodwin 2008). What we are witnessing today is the natural conclusion of this tendency: the death by asphyxiation of an unwanted discipline; a smothered mate. The dismissal of historians of economic ideas by the 'true and real' economists is by now a well-established fact. Mark Blaug's 2001 article in the *Journal of Economic Perspectives* had the telling title 'No History of Ideas, Please, We're Economists', while Roy Weintraub (2007) opens his 'Economic Science Wars' article with the observation that 'It is not news that the history of economics is disesteemed by most economists. There have been almost annual discussions at professional meetings about the institutional role of the history of economics.' Weintraub (2002) also edited a HOPE annual supplement in which this trend has been documented.

So, is it time to ditch HET for good? Is it an antediluvian fossil, whose teaching distracts students and professors from doing 'real' economic science? Should we pack our bags and move into the safer haven of History and Philosophy of Science Graduate Departments? In a well-argued and passionate article, Professor Alessandro Roncaglia steps in to defend HET. Professor of Economics at the University 'La Sapienza' in Rome, Roncaglia is a political economist and an eminent member of the HET community. His textbook, *La ricchezza delle idee: Storia del pensiero economico*, [Rome, Laterza, 2001, 6th edition 2012] won the 2003 Jérome Adolphe Blanqui Award from the European Society for the History of Economic Thought. Its English version *The Wealth of Ideas: A History of Economic Thought* was published by Cambridge University Press in 2005. The first chapter of that treatise provides an important background for a better understanding of the article at hand. His 1996 article in the *European Journal of the History of Economic Thought* delivers a strong advocacy of the necessity of HET. On a personal note,

Roncaglia's book is the main text I use in my graduate courses in HET at UADPhilEcon, the doctoral programme in economics at the University of Athens, perhaps one of the very few doctoral programmes where HET is mandatory.

First, let me make clear what is at stake here. Nobody wants to abolish HET as a scientific discipline. The question is (a) whether HET should be part of undergraduate or graduate curricula, i.e., whether it is necessary for the *training* of economists and (b) whether HET is a proper subdiscipline of economics. Roncaglia answers affirmatively to both questions. I concur.

Roncaglia presents the opening salvo fired at HET by Donald Gordon (1965, p. 126), that '[e]conomic theory [...] finds no necessity for including its history as a part of professional training'. He notes that not only has this become the mainstream tenet, but that tenet was already held in the 1930s, at least by the top professionals of the field. It is, perhaps, that objections against teaching the history of any discipline are raised in general when the brave new world of the new science wants to discard the teachings of the past, and proceed unencumbered on the new path leading chiefly to the truth. Examples abound: Jean d'Alembert, in his *Essay on the elements of philosophy,* speaks of 'L'Histoire des Sophismes' (1760, p. 12). Adam Smith wrote of 'the exploded systems and obsolete prejudices' that 'found shelter and protection' in 'learned societies [...] after they had been hunted out of every other corner of the world' (1776/1976, V.i.f., p. 772). Jean Baptiste Say (1829, p. 561) though having produced his *Abbreviated history of the progress of political economy,* asks 'what can we gain by collecting absurd opinions [and] discredited doctrines? It would be both pointless and cumbersome to exhume them'. His answer for writing a small HET is that 'any kind of history is entitled to flatter curiosity, we get to know about the processes of the human mind; an error that is unveiled prevents us from committing it again, its discussion reveals and consolidates the foundations of a truth, and finally, when the principles of science are still debated in some respects, its history admits controversies that shed light upon the disputed points and even upon the whole of science.' Arthur C. Pigou (1902, p. 374), reviewing Hannah Robie Sewall's *The Theory of Value before Adam Smith,* even while praising her erudition speaks of 'antiquarian researches ... in studying confessedly inadequate solutions offered centuries ago'. Hugh Dalton (1920, p. 33) speaks of 'the wrong opinions of dead men'. Roncaglia may be right that 'in the 1930s, [...] economists belonging to the then dominant Marshallian tradition such as John Hicks and Dennis Robertson argued that there was no point in wasting time reading the classical economists'. But the thirties were at the heart of the Golden Age of HET (Goodwin 2008). It was in 1934–5 when Wesley C. Mitchell delivered his Columbia Lectures which constitute possibly the best defence HET has ever had (Mitchell 1949). Even J.R. Hicks – who may have not been well versed in the

Ricardian tradition, as Roncaglia ably shows – had produced a first-rate piece of HET in his 1934 article on Walras (Hicks 1934).[16]

Professor Roncaglia produces the evidence of the decline of HET in academic curricula and offers two tentative explanations: the first is that the axiomatisation of economics hypostatises the assumptions and, once these have been accepted, there is no need to discuss their historical roots. Indeed, mainstream economics is characterised by an ahistorical approach, refusing to accept that its subject matter changes with the times and that this eternal individual – the economic agent – does not exist in cosmic limbo, but is socially constructed. Having jettisoned economic history, it is only natural for mainstream theory to harbour distaste for all history – particularly of the discipline itself – and for all non-mathematically formulated arguments. A solid logical construct, however, does not necessarily imply an aversion to history. Sraffa's *Prelude to a Critique of Economic Theory* (1960) is, in a sense, quite axiomatic but we count great historians of economic thought among his followers. Economists operating within the axiomatic tradition also turned the tools of their science to axiomatic interpretations of past doctrines.[17]

Roncaglia provides a second explanation for the declining role of HET: the major experience of the Cold War, 'with a widespread (and, as a matter of fact, largely erroneous) identification of Classical with Marxian economics, where HET was perceived as the Trojan horse to infiltrate Western culture with anti-capitalist ideas'. This is a plausible explanation, but I believe that the true ideological battle between neoclassical economic theory and classical political economy was born with the marginalist revolution, indeed even before that. In neoclassical theory, economics was sterilised from its social content; social classes gave place to consumers/owners of the factors of production[18] and entrepreneurs. Abstract focus shifted from production to exchange [the *catallactics* of Bishop Whately (1831, p. 6)]. More importantly, a labour theory of value, however unwittingly or implicitly, had the political and ideological implication that since labour creates value it is the rightful claimant to the whole produce. No matter that Henry

---

[16] This was not the only excursion of Hicks to HET. For an indicative list of eminent economists who have engaged in HET during the golden age see Goodwin (2008, p.8).
[17] Two eminent examples of mainstream economists working within the mathematical axiomatic tradition who took inspiration from the classical authors to produce first-rate work that is both economic theory and HET are Michio Morishima and Takashi Negishi (See Kurz 2011). It is true, however, that economists trained in the axiomatic tradition when they do HET they usually opt for a rational reconstruction of economic doctrines of the past, 'filling in' assumptions that the original authors never made in order to provide what they think is a coherent mathematical model. [For a discussion of the Lakatosian notion of rational reconstruction see Waterman (2003) and Marcuzzo (2008)]. It seems that when rational reconstruction fell out of fashion and historical reconstruction became the accepted norm, many economists working within the axiomatic tradition felt that they did not want to have anything to do with HET. My own view is that it is the possibility of excluding contending paradigms that is responsible for the decline of HET rather than the axiomatic method as such.
[18] The worker in Walras (1926, L.18 §184) is described as the 'holder of personal faculties' [*détenteur des facultés personnelles*].

Sidgwick (1887, p. 57) referred contemptuously to 'those Socialists who have perverted Ricardo's inconsistency into an argument against the remuneration of capitalists'. By the end of the 19th century, authors making this assertion were numerous enough to make a distinct group worthy of a monograph (Menger 1899/1970, see Theocarakis 2010). Eugen von Böhm-Bawerk (1884/1921, I (XII), p. 318) argued that the 'exploitation theory' (*Ausbeutungstheorie*) 'stood at the cradle of modern Socialism and has grown up along with it; and to-day it forms the theoretical centre around which move the forces of attack and defence in the struggle of organising human society.' I agree with Professor Roncaglia that the identification of classical political economy with Marxism is erroneous, but the prodigal son is there, and the issues raised by classical political economy were not seen as scientifically neutral by what came to be the dominant side of the profession. As to how that came to be is, of course, another major question. After all, if you are going to do HET properly you cannot exclude Marx and Marxism – or post-Ricardian and utopian socialists for that matter – and opt only for those subjects that do not question the foundations of capitalism.[19] 'One learns it is better to *avoid* an argument than to win one' [Paul A. Samuelson, quoted in Mirowski (2013a, p. 7)]. One who does not learn this, is one soon to be excluded by the ones who do.

Roncaglia then examines three reasons provided in the literature for including HET in the core curriculum: (a) a straightforwardly pedagogical reason (Gordon), (b) an aristocratic/elitist notion of scholarship (Viner), an amulet against the perils of becoming an *idiot-savant* and (c) the 'lumber room' function for getting new ideas (Schumpeter), a source of inspiration. Indeed, as Roncaglia notes, in his magisterial *History of Economic Analysis* (1954, p. 3), Schumpeter has provided most of these reasons: 'The gains with which we may hope to emerge from [HET] can be displayed under three heads: pedagogical advantages, new ideas, and insights into the ways of the human mind'.

Roncaglia does not deny the usefulness of these views, but does not consider them to be the main reason why HET should be taught. I agree. Take the pedagogical reason first: the value of HET may be a matter of 'cost benefit analysis', as Stigler argued (1969, pp. 229-230). But, as Roncaglia correctly points out, 'HET's pedagogical usefulness is reduced whenever there is discontinuity in the development of the analytical toolbox with no change in the underlying worldview, as in fact was the case after the Second World War with the publication of Samuelson's *Foundations* (1947).'[20] Do graduate students understand Mas-Colell *et al.* (1995) *Microeconomic Theory* better by

---

[19] In Marcuzzo's (2008, Fig. 3) tabulation of past authors as article subjects in HET journals listed in *EconLit* the top five authors accounting for almost half of the authors studied are (in that order) Smith, Keynes, Hayek, Marx and Veblen.

[20] The *Foundations* may seem an odd choice since Samuelson himself was a prolific author of HET papers (e.g., Medema and Waterman 2010). But it is not. Samuelson, like many economists who adopt the cumulative point of view, quite often creates rational rather than historical reconstructions of older theories (Blaug 1990).

being taught the labour theory of value? Sadly not, since there is no single mention of the word 'labour' in its almost 1000 pages. Second, the 'scholarship' argument may hold true for the economists themselves, but perhaps not for their theory. Leijonhufvud (2007) has suggested that HET courses are treated like courses in dining etiquette in military academies. An officer should also be a gentleman, but his manners are not related to his tactical acumen in the battlefield. It is nonetheless true, that much is being lost from a lack of general education in HET in the formation of economists. The arrogance of the ignorant that characterises many of our profession can be annoying. Third, the 'inspiration' argument may also appear as somewhat weak at first sight. Inspiration may come from a variety of sources: a falling apple or a Petri dish with mould. Still, there is no better source of inspiration than the doctrines of the great minds of the past.

Professor Roncaglia acknowledges the importance of the reasons given above but he argues that the importance of HET lies in its ability (a) to help us better understand our own concepts and (b) to promote the scientific debate between contending paradigms. These two reasons are distinct from each other. HET is good practice even for orthodox economics. The mainstream view, however, implies a 'cumulative' methodological approach, viz., that 'the provisional point of arrival of contemporary economics incorporates all previous contributions in an improved way'.[21] The 'cumulative' theory may work by demolishing previous theories, or by 'improving' on them. Thus, while Jevons (1879, p. xlix) in his criticism of the Ricardian economists argued that they 'have been living in a fool's paradise', Marshall (1920, V, xv, §5, p. 503) held that 'the foundations of the theory as they were left by Ricardo remain intact; that much has been added to them, and that very much has been built upon them, but that little has been taken from them'.

According to Roncaglia, it is the often implicit positivism of mainstream economics that dictates this cumulative approach. This approach, however, is not confined to either neoclassical theory or to positivism. Teleology is another source: in his *History of Economic Thought* (1926/1979) for example, Isaac Ilych Rubin discusses pre-Marxist economic thought as imperfect attempts to arrive at Marx's theory. The historical approach of Marxism – the critique of bourgeois political economy – however, thrives in HET. In grand theoretical schemes, the history of thought serves another purpose, viz., to provide a framework in which all previous theories can be explained in relation to the new theoretical solution offered. This can be the case of very dissimilar works such as Marx's *Capital* (1867) and Böhm-Bawerk's *Capital and Interest* (1884).

Roncaglia takes from Schumpeter the notion of 'conceptualisation', namely 'to verbalise the vision or to conceptualise it in such a way that its elements take their places,

---

[21] This is exemplified in Pantaleoni's (1897, p. 4) simile of 'the growth of a snowball that runs down the slope of a mountain picking up more snow, and the surface of which represents the unknown'.

with names attached to them that facilitate recognition and manipulation, in a more or less orderly schema or picture'. According to Roncaglia, all mainstream views share the same vision and conceptualisation before proceeding to model-building and to the application of these models to the interpretation of economic reality. By doing so, mainstream theory shuns alternative conceptualisations/paradigms. Roncaglia provides as an example the difference between the classical and the marginalist conceptualisations of the economy.

I fully agree with Professor Roncaglia that alternative conceptualisations of the economy should form part of the training of an economist. I also agree with him that HET is very useful in the elucidation of the 'concepts utilised in economic theorising' even within the confines of a single approach, mainstream or not. I also wholeheartedly endorse his argument that HET is 'essential [...] for serious debate between contending paradigms'. Scientific debates between contending paradigms forge better weapons and keep the interest of teachers and students alive.[22] My objection is that we should not mince words and carry the argument to its logical conclusions: teaching HET is not enough. We should create a more open academia where faculty members can follow alternative paradigms. In such an academia HET would play a prominent role as a tool of debate.

Mainstream economic theory did a very poor job in predicting or explaining the 2008 global financial crisis. Roncaglia (2010) himself has written a book on the subject. Even worse were the orthodox recipes for getting out of the crisis. Alternative paradigms should have been, and indeed have been, very useful in remedying this. At present there is a very marked trend in academia to exclude all dissenting voices. This is done not through scientific debate but by controlling the means of the academic future of dissenters. Quantification through rigged dice blocks the promotion of dissenters. Citation and impact factors act against those of minority opinion. Demoting journals that host alternative views makes certain that those who hold them will not reach the appropriate level of seniority to influence things academic and serves as a warning to graduate students and junior faculty in their choice of research. Homogenisation of curricula through the Bologna process in Europe and ranking quantophrenia everywhere, put dissenters in their place. It is this process of silencing dissent that is mainly responsible for the trend to exclude HET from academic curricula. At least Odysseus tied himself to the mast of his ship in order to hear the song of the sirens, even if he was unable to join them. In modern academia his ears would have been plugged.

---

[22] This is, of course, not confined to economics. Albert Einstein has written – with Leopold Infeld – a history of physics, admittedly for the lay reader, in which he wanted to defend his realist approach to physics against quantum mechanics (Einstein and Infeld 1938). The authors state at the end of the Preface that they wish to give to the reader 'some idea of the eternal struggle of the inventive human mind for a fuller understanding of the laws governing physical phenomena.'

Mainstream economists see HET as the last institutional bastion of alternative or 'heterodox' theoretical approaches. They feel that its teaching is heterodoxy's last attempt to enter the curriculum [undergraduate or graduate] precisely at a time when they have been so successful in excluding them from the *métier*. Their mistrust is enhanced by the number of historians of economic thought who are sympathetic to non-mainstream views (Lodewijks 2003, Weintraub 2007, p. 277 *et seq.*). It is also official: the *American Economic Association* renamed the JEL one digit classification code B from 'History of Economic Thought and Methodology' to 'History of Economic Thought, Methodology, and Heterodox Approaches' adding the classification 'B5 - Current Heterodox Approaches', i.e., 'HET and all that'.

This connection between HET and heterodoxy is not the fault of HET as a discipline. It reflects the fact that non-orthodox economists have been chased away from orthodox economic departments to 'lesser' disciplines or, occasionally, to Business Schools, where interestingly, future managers still seek relevance in order to run their businesses. In most economics departments these days the only place where students can find out about Ricardo, Marx, Keynes and Sraffa is in HET courses. Now mainstream economists want to sever the tie altogether and throw the unwanted baby out with the bathwater. They say that there are two kinds of economics: 'good economics' and 'bad economics'. They presumably teach the former (Marglin 2011). It is interesting to note that Schumpeter, whose *History of Economic Analysis* (1954) is mildly cumulativist or Whiggish, provides a fourth reason for teaching HET.

> Although it is possible nevertheless—as I shall try to show—to speak for every epoch of established professional opinion on scientific topics and although this opinion has often stood the test of being proof against strong differences in political views, we cannot speak with as much confidence about it as can physicists or mathematicians. In consequence we cannot, or at least we do not, trust one another to sum up 'the state of the science' in an equally satisfactory manner. And the obvious remedy for the shortcomings of summarizing works is the study of doctrinal history: much more than in, say, physics is it true in economics that modern problems, methods, and results cannot be fully understood without some knowledge of how economists have come to reason as they do.

In other words: 'Put your trust in God; but mind to keep your powder dry'.

I find the connection between HET and heterodox approaches a pity for the discipline. It is, however, collateral damage. Not only is it a generalisation which is not true for a very large numbers of HET practitioners, but it is a disservice to orthodox and heterodox economists alike. Mainstream economists seeing reds under the HET bed are deprived of the benefits of the discipline; while, instead of going on with their own agenda, heterodox economists are forced to spend too much time 'in the lumber room'. Now the lumber room is in danger of being shut down. If the practice of alternative paradigms becomes the province of some dedicated academic outcasts, we all have to lose. 'If the salt have lost his savour, wherewith shall it be salted?' At the moment heterodox economics is on HET life-support. It should be a first step of revitalising it. But if the bond is entirely severed, intuitions from the 'lumber room' cannot resurface even as 'old wine in new bottles'. Moreover, the false notion that HET is a second-rate discipline creates the impression that HET is anybody's game, where junior or retired members of academia can 'moonlight' with papers that boost their CVs or keep them active, clogging HET journal editors with ahistorical articles that often 'haruspicate or scry'.

With its alternative conceptualisations, HET destroys yet another myth which is reinforced through the ritual of paying lip service to a simplistic positivism. Economics has supposedly come of age and is now a truly positive science. It is done through hypothesis testing and falsifiability as a poor imitation of a 19th century physics paradigm (Mirowski 1989). The critique of positivism is now standard in other sciences, but absent in economics, even though – as Bruce Caldwell (2013) has so ably shown – this is only an affectation. Indeed, you cannot trust a baby with an Occam's razor.

The difference between the positive or natural sciences and the social sciences or humanities goes back at least to Galileo Galilei. In his *Dialogue concerning the two chief world systems, Ptolemaic and Copernican* (1632), Galileo argues that in the *studi umani* 'in which neither true nor false exists, one might trust in subtlety of mind and readiness of tongue and in the greater experience of the writers', whereas 'in the natural sciences, whose conclusions are true and necessary and have nothing to do with human will, one must take care not to place oneself in the defense of error; for here a thousand Demostheneses and a thousand Aristotles would be left in the lurch by every mediocre wit who happened to hit upon the truth for himself' (1967, 53-54 ; 1632, 45-6). Mainstream economists pose as a latter-day Salvatius putting the truth into the pathetic head of heterodox Simplicius. Weintraub (2007) has used the debates following C.P. Snow's *Two Cultures* lecture and the *Science Wars* episode to explain how eventually both HET *and* methodology have suffered in the process. It is clear that it is the *ideology* of the two culture divide (Smith 2005, p. 108) that has made its mark here. Heterodox economists and historians of economic thought are not the 'literary intellectuals' stereotyped by C.P. Snow and ridiculed by Alan Sokal.

What, however, Weintraub's (2007) analysis shows is that historians of economic thought should turn their own tools on their own discipline and provide a historical explanation of this gradual, but significant, erosion of HET in the consciousness and perceptions of economists themselves. It is time for a meta-HET: Craufurd D. Goodwin

(2008) and Weintraub (2007) are good examples of this. This history of HET shows that the Golden Age of our discipline – from after the First World War to the 1960s – was not only the age when HET thrived and when the best economists contributed to it as part of the general discourse in economics, but was also the age where competing paradigms fought it out to produce a better theory that would substitute the discredited theories of the complacent Victorian certainties and the harmonious operation of the markets. HET is nowadays ostracised because a solidified orthodoxy excludes alternative conceptualisations even after the mainstream theory has failed dismally in explaining the crisis. The question that has to be answered – in historical and political, as well as in doctrinal and technical, terms – is why, *after* the global financial and economic meltdown, we do not see a revitalisation of the competition between alternative paradigms and a revival of HET as we did after the Great Crash? This time is really different (Mirowski 2013).

Well, does knowledge of HET make you a better economist? Mainstream economists should realise, like Horatio, that 'there are more things in heaven and earth, […] than are dreamt of in [their] philosophy'. Even if they exorcise the ghost of heterodoxy, alternative paradigms are not dead in society. And in public discourse, mainstream theorists should be able to engage in dialogue, which is impossible if they only know their own small formally constructed universe. Moreover, if these mainstream economists had delivered what they promised they would, maybe there would be cause for pride in what they are doing and disdain for those who question their methods. But they did not. And even if they were quick to revert to their old ways, and refuse to re-examine their conceptualisations or their vision, intellectual honesty dictates they should. HET is the first step in such a direction. If they cannot do better on their own, they can pick from the riches of past theories the elements necessary for a re-examination of what they are doing.

In assessing their hypotheses and theories, economists should be aware that looking at t-statistics is not enough (Ziliak and McCloskey 2008). In a social science such as economics, economists should acknowledge that 'internal' reasons are not the only driving force for rejecting specific hypotheses. They may pretend that internal consistency and meeting the test of reality is what they do when rejecting heterodox theories, but a good dose of HET will teach them to be more humble. By rejecting HET, they are forced to accept an obsolete, as well as false, methodology which makes them bad scientists. It is in fact curious that economists do not wish to reflect on the history of their own science, how it has been developed and how and why new avenues have been explored. Athena may have jumped fully armed and grown-up out of the head of Zeus; science never does. It is only an Orwellian Ministry of Truth that constantly erases the tracks of the past (Mirowski 2004). Reliance on a mechanical paradigm of a rational automaton may simplify things and give the impression of a positive science, but only through HET can we explore the fullness and subtlety of alternative models of society and get a glimpse of the 'path not taken' or the way in which the negative edifice guarded by Cerberus has been built, where live the questions that may not be asked. It is only when, in a HET course, we examine the attempts of the philosophers and economists of the past to explain the economic and social reality of their time that we can comprehend in full the subject matter of our science. Blind men should grope the elephant from various angles before they understand the nature of the beast. This is perhaps the best pedagogical lesson that will motivate interest in budding economists and illuminate their role in the enterprise called science.

As an anti-climax to my peroration – and it is here where pragmatism steps in – I would argue that we cannot reach the economic truth within closed theoretical systems (Varoufakis *et al.* 2011). We have to be judicious, selective, and methodologically open. At best, we can use our rhetoric to enlighten and inform those who can be persuaded and who will engage in dialogue with us in our search for relevance. Knowledge of HET can then be very useful, since it can provide arguments – perhaps in newly stated forms – and show that the victory of doctrinaire views is not related to their inherent truth. Let alternative conceptualisations bloom. I thank Alessandro Roncaglia for making this point powerfully clear.

Acknowledgements

I wish to thank Roy Weintraub and Michalis Psalidopoulos for their comments on a previous draft and George E. Krimpas for going through both drafts. The usual disclaimer applies.

References

Alembert, Jean le Rond d' (1760) 'Essai sur les élémens de philosophie, ou sur les principes des connoissances humaines', in : *Mélanges de littérature, d'histoire et de philosophie*, vol. 4 (Amsterdam: Aux dépens de la Compagnie), new edition, pp. 1-292.

Blaug, Mark (1990) 'On the Historiography of Economics', *Journal of the History of Economic Thought*, 12 (1), pp. 27-37.

Blaug, Mark (2001) 'No History of Ideas, Please, We're Economists', *Journal of Economic Perspectives*, 15 (1), pp. 145-164.

Böhm-Bawerk, Eugen von (1884/1921) *Kapital und Kapitalzins. Erste Abtheilung: Geschichte und Kritik der Kapitalzins-Theorien* (Jena: Gustav Fischer). 4th edition.

Caldwell, Bruce (2013) 'Presidential Address: Of Positivism and the History of Economic Thought', *Southern Economic Journal*, 79 (4), pp. 753–767.

Dalton, Hugh (1920) *Some Aspects of the Inequality of Incomes in Modern Communities* (London: George Routledge and New York: E.P. Dutton).

Einstein, Albert and Leopold Infeld (1938) *The Evolution of Physics: The Growth of Ideas from the Early Concepts to Relativity and Quanta* (Cambridge: University Press).

Galilei, Galileo (1632) *Dialogo [...] sopra i due massimi sistemi del mondo, tolemaico, e copernicano* (Florence: Gio. Battista Landini).

Galilei, Galileo (1967) *Dialogue Concerning the Two Chief World Systems, Ptolemaic and Copernican*, translated by Stillman Drake (Berkeley, CA: University of California Press), 2nd edition.

Gayer, Ted (2002) 'Graduate Studies in the History of Economic Thought', in: E. Roy Weintraub (ed.), *The Future of the History of Economics* (Durham, NC: Duke University Press), pp. 35–61.

Goodwin, Craufurd D. (2008) 'History of Economic Thought', in: Steven N. Durlauf and Lawrence E. Blume (eds), *The New Palgrave Dictionary of Economics Online* (Basingstoke, UK and New York: Palgrave Macmillan), accessed 30/9/ 2013, <http://dictionaryofeconomic.com/article?id=pde2008_H000174>, doi:10.1057/9780230226203.0741.

Gordon, Donald F. (1965) 'The Role of the History of Economic Thought in the Understanding of Modern Economic Theory', *American Economic Review*, 55 (1/2), pp. 119-127.

Hicks, J. R. (1934) 'Léon Walras', *Econometrica*, 2 (4), pp. 338-348.

Jevons, W. Stanley (1879) *The Theory of Political Economy* (London: Macmillan), 2nd edition.

Johnson, Samuel (1755) 'Lexicographer' entry in: *A Dictionary of English Language* (London: Printed by W. Strahan, for J. and P. Knapton [*et al.*]).

Kurz, Heinz D. (2011) 'The Contributions of Two Eminent Japanese Scholars to the Development of Economic Theory: Michio Morishima and Takashi Negishi', in: Heinz D. Kurz, Tamotsu Nishizawa and Keith Tribe (eds), *The Dissemination of Economic Ideas*, (Cheltenham: E. Elgar), pp. 337-364.

Leijonhufvud, Axel (2007) *The 3rd Public Lecture in Memory of Kosmas Psychopaidis*, (Athens: UADPhilEcon, National and Kapodistrian University of Athens)

Lodewijks, John (2003) 'Research in the History of Economic Thought as a Vehicle for the Defense and Criticism of Orthodox Economics', in: Warren J. Samuels, Jeff E. Biddle and John B. Davis (eds), *Companion to the History of Economic Thought* (Malden, MA and Oxford, UK: Blackwell Publishing), pp. 655-668.

Marglin, Stephen (2011) 'Heterodox Economics: Alternatives to Mankiw's Ideology', *Occupy Harvard Teach-In #1*, 7 December, Online available at http://www.youtube.com/watch?v=Pf0-E8X-GHo

Marshall, Alfred (1920) *Principles of Economics: An Introductory Volume* (London: Macmillan), 8th edition.

Marcuzzo, Maria Cristina (2008) 'Is History of Economic Thought a "Serious" Subject?', *Erasmus Journal for Philosophy and Economics*, 1 (1), pp. 107-123.

Marx, Karl (1867) *Das Kapital, Kritik der politischen Ökonomie: Erster Band*, in: *Karl Marx – Friedrich Engels Werke*, edited by the Institut für Marxismus-Leninismus beim ZK der SED (Berlin (DDR): Dietz Verlag), vol. 23 (1962).

Mas-Colell, Andreu, Michael D. Whinston, and Jerry R. Green (1995) *Microeconomic Theory* (New York and Oxford: Oxford University Press).

Medema, Steven G., and Anthony M.C. Waterman (2010) 'Paul Anthony Samuelson: Historian of Economic Thought', *History of Economic Ideas*, 18 (3), pp. 67-86

Menger, Anton (1891) *Das Recht auf den vollen Arbeitsertrag in geschichtlicher Darstellung* (Stuttgart: Cotta), 2nd edition.

Mirowski, Philip (1989) *More Heat Than Light* (Cambridge: Cambridge University Press).

Mirowski, Philip (2004) 'Philosophizing with a Hammer: Reply to Binmore, Davis and Klaes', Book Review Symposium, *Journal of Economic Methodology*, 11 (4), pp. 499–513.

Mirowski, Philip (2013) *Never Let a Serious Crisis Go to Waste: How Neoliberalism Survived the Financial Meltdown* (London: Verso).

Mirowski, Philip (2013a) '2012 HES Presidential Address: Does the Victor Enjoy the Spoils? Paul Samuelson as Historian of Economics', *Journal of the History of Economic Thought*, 35 (1), pp. 1-17.

Mitchell, Wesley C. (1949) *Lecture Notes on Types of Economic Theory* (New York: A. M. Kelley).

Pantaleoni, Maffeo (1897) 'Del carattere delle divergenze d'opinione esistenti tra economisti' (Introductory lecture to the course on economics delivered at the University of Geneva) in: *id.*, (1904), *Scritti varii di economia* (Milan [etc.]: Remo Sandron).

Pigou, A. C. (1902) '*The Theory of Value before Adam Smith*. by Hannah Robie Sewall', *Economic Journal,* 12 (47), pp. 374-375

Plato (1924) *Plato: Laches; Protagoras; Memo; Euthydemus*, translated by W.R.M. Lamb (Cambridge, MA: Harvard University Press).

Roncaglia, Alessandro (1996) 'Why Should Economists Study the History of Economic Thought?', *European Journal of the History of Economic Thought*, 3 (2), pp. 296-309.

Roncaglia, Alessandro (2001) *La ricchezza delle idee: Storia del pensiero economico*, (Rome: Laterza), 6th edition 2012.

Roncaglia, Alessandro (2005) *The Wealth of Ideas: A History of Economic Thought* (Cambridge: Cambridge University Press).

Roncaglia, Alessandro (2010) *Why Economists Got It Wrong: The Crisis and Its Cultural Roots* (London and New York: Anthem Press). [Italian edition: *Economisti che sbagliano. Le radici culturali della crisi* (Rome: Laterza) 2010].

Rubin, Isaac Ilych (1979) *A History of Economic Thought*, translated and edited by Donald Filtzer (London: Ink Links). 1st Russian edition 1926.

Say, Jean-Baptiste (1829) 'Histoire abrégée des progrès de l'économie politique', in: *id.* (1840), *Cours complet d'économie politique pratique* (Brussels : Société Belge de Librairie), pp. 561-576. 2nd edition.

Schumpeter, Joseph A. (1954) *History of Economic Analysis* (London: George Allen & Unwin).

Sidgwick, Henry (1887) *The Principles of Political Economy* (London: Macmillan), 2nd edition.

Smith, Adam (1776/1976), *An Inquiry into the Nature and Causes of the Wealth of Nations*, R. H. Campbell and A. S. Skinner (general editors), W. B. Todd (textual editor), *Glasgow Edition of the Works and Correspondence of Adam Smith* (Oxford: Clarendon), vol. 2.

Smith, Barbara Herrnstein (2005) *Scandalous Knowledge: Science, Truth and the Human* (Edinburgh: Edinburgh University Press).

Sraffa, Piero (1960) *Production of Commodities by Means of Commodities: Prelude to a Critique of Economic Theory* (Cambridge: Cambridge University Press).

Stigler, George J. (1969) 'Does Economics Have a Useful Past?', *History of Political Economy*, 1 (2), pp. 217-230.

Theocarakis, Nicholas J. (2010) 'Metamorphoses: The Concept of Labour in the History of Political Economy', *Economic and Labour Relations Review*, 20 (2), pp. 7–38.

Varoufakis, Yanis, Joseph Halevi and Nicholas J. Theocarakis (2011) *Modern Political Economics: Making Sense of the Post-2008 World* (London and New York: Routledge).

Walras, Léon (1926) *Éléments d'économie politique pure: ou, Théorie de la richesse sociale* (Paris : R. Pichon & R. Durand-Auzias), 'édition définitive'.

Waterman, A. M. C. (2003) 'Mathematical Modeling as an Exegetical Tool: Rational Reconstruction', in: Warren J. Samuels, Jeff E. Biddle and John B. Davis (eds), *Companion to the History of Economic Thought* (Malden, MA and Oxford, UK: Blackwell Publishing), pp. 553-570.

Weintraub, E. Roy (2007) 'Economic Science Wars', *Journal of the History of Economic Thought*, 29 (3), pp. 267-282.

Weintraub, E. Roy (ed.) (2002) *The Future of the History of Economics* (Durham, NC: Duke University Press), *History of Political Economy*, Annual Supplement.

Whately, Richard (1831) *Introductory Lectures on Political Economy* (London: B. Fellowes).

Ziliak, Stephen T. and Deirdre N. McCloskey (2008) *The Cult of Statistical Significance: How the Standard Error Costs Us Jobs, Justice, and Lives* (Ann Arbor, MI: University of Michigan Press).

SUGGESTED CITATION:

Theocarakis, N. (2014) 'A commentary on Alessandro Roncaglia's paper: "Should the History of Economic Thought be Included in Undergraduate Curricula?"'. *Economic Thought*, 3.1, pp. 10-20.
http://www.worldeconomicsassociation.org/files/journals/economicthought/WEA-ET-3-1-Theocarakis.pdf

From Rational Choice to Reflexivity: Learning from Sen, Keynes, Hayek, Soros, and most of all, from Darwin

Alex Rosenberg, Department of Philosophy, Duke University, USA
alexrose@duke.edu

Abstract

This paper identifies the major failings of mainstream economics and the rational choice theory it relies upon. These failures were identified by the four figures mentioned in the title: economics treats agents as rational fools; by the time the long run equilibrium arrives, we are all dead; the social, political and economic institutions that meet most urgent human needs most effectively could not have been the result of rational choice, but their 'spontaneous order' needs to be explained; human uncertainty and reflexivity prohibit a predictively useful rational choice approach to human affairs, and even limit its role in institution design. What unifies the perspectives of all four of these critics of neoclassical economics, however, is their implicit reliance or on need for a Darwinian perspective on human affairs.

Keywords: uncertainty, reflexivity, function, strategies, Darwin, Soros, frequency-dependent selection

1. Introduction

Rational Choice models (hereafter RCT or, for fun, Rat Choice), and the microeconomist's approach to employing them are in the ascendancy among social scientists. Political scientists have been expounding it for 25 years. In the last decade or so its application has extended to experimental social psychology and even neuroscience. Among economists rational choice models have been the only game in town for at least a century.

As is so often the case in the social sciences, this influence – hegemony might be a better word – is more a matter of fashion than achievement. It is mostly the result of theoretical tractability, mathematical elegance, and ideologically convenient rationalisation. It certainly is not owing to the predictive success of theories and models inspired by rational choice theory and the way in which economists employ it. Why is it that Rat Choice is so appealing despite the absence of much of a pay-off to using it?

The strength of the temptation to adopt the RCT approaches to explain human affairs is overwhelming. Introspection tells each of us, you and me, that we are rational creatures, who choose among alternatives on the basis of our beliefs and desires – in Rat Choice speak – our expectations and preferences. Similarly, we explain other people's behaviour by *interpreting* it, that is, making guesses about what desires and beliefs they must have had that worked together to bring about their behaviour. RCT is just folk psychology formalised. Since we can't shake folk psychology, we are suckers for Rat Choice. It has all the allure of our most psychologically satisfying stories. The stern admonition of science – that the mere reduction of feelings of curiosity is no mark of explanatory power – falls on our deaf ears. But we had better be able to give it up, if we want a useful social science.

The problems of RCT are four fold: Sen's problem of rational fools, Keynes' problem about the long run, Hayek's problem of spontaneous order, and Soros' problem of reflexivity/uncertainty.[23]

2. Sen's Problem of 'Rational Fools'

This is Amartya Sen's (1977) label for the charge that RCT is not only incapable of explaining a great deal of the most characteristic of human behaviours. What is worse, Sen argues, it would be foolish to substitute the choices RCT dictates for the ones we actually make.

Rat Choice is surprised by the degree to which people cooperate, mutually provide public goods – ones that are nonexcludable and non-rivalrous. The source of this cooperation Sen identified as their 'commitment' (1977). RCT almost always recommends free riding, and other strategies that unravel cooperative institutions. But these institutions persist. In order to reconcile itself with reality RCT must make unreasonable *ad hoc* assumptions about the shape of preference curves, and equally *ad hoc* ones about probabilistic expectations. RCT continues to struggle in the quest to explain away three facts: the frequency with which we succeed in providing ourselves with public goods; the frequency with which we honour norms that inhibit self-interest; and the net-costs we willingly impose on ourselves to police their violation.

Economists didn't start to take Sen's critique seriously until it began to emerge from computer simulations in game theory and human experiments in cognitive social

---

[23] No one should suppose that the argument to follow constitutes a full or even balanced account of the contributions to economic theory of the four figures. This paper is not a contribution to the scholarship of their work. I shamelessly pluck from their manifold contributions themes that work together in proving a telling account of the limits of received mainstream neoclassical economics.

psychology. Even now, these two sources of evidence are met with much resistance by mainstream economists. Sen's insight was the need for a richer psychology than Rat Choice allows, one that has room for commitment, among other features. A decade after Sen's original paper, Robert Frank (1988) advanced this insight in detail. In *Passion within Reason* he argued that there are a variety of crucial social-interaction problems people regularly solve in ways RCT cannot accommodate. Rational choice theory makes honesty the best policy, except where you can get away with dishonesty. In a straight contest between unconditional honesty and RCT's qualified honesty, the latter wins and unravels most of our social institutions. If we really were Rat choosers, we'd still be in Hobbes' state of nature. We aren't, so RCT must be wrong about the most fundamental facts of human psychology and social life. Sen, Frank, and a generation of cognitive social psychologists following them, have shown that human affairs are driven not by Rat Choice but by emotions harnessed to norms of fairness, equality, and real non-opportunistic altruism.

This work has combined with another line of research to undermine, if not unravel, RCT. Start with the most profound regress problem Rat Choice faces, one first identified by Sidney Winter (1975) and Jon Elster (1978): to make a rational choice you need to have correct expectations – accurate information about alternatives. Acquiring knowledge about alternatives costs resources and presents an optimisation problem. How much should you spend to acquire the information you need? This is a problem for RCT. How to solve the problem of figuring out how much to spend in a particular case? Use RTC? How to solve the problem of figuring out how much to spend to figure out the problem of how much to spend to acquire the information in the first place, and so on...

How, in fact, does this regress get cut short? Herbert Simon answered the question in the general case even before Winter and Elster articulated the problem. Humans don't maximise, as RCT requires: they satisfice. This is an insight Tversky and Kahnemann (2011) developed into a Nobel Prize winning insight about the role of heuristics in decision making, what Gigerenzer calls fast and frugal cognitive strategies for making choices. Humans are as fully committed to these cognitive norms as they are to the emotionally driven moral norms that prevent us from making rational fools of ourselves. (The relevance of this work to Sen's earlier independent insights was not lost on Kahneman, 2003, p. 152.)

RCT started out life as a psychological theory, an account of how people make choices. Just ask Jevons (1877) or Edgeworth (1895, 2003) or Wicksteed (1910). By the time Milton Friedman wrote 'The methodology of positive economics' he, and his more farsighted colleagues (for example Gary Becker), had recognised they needed quite a different rationale for their attachment to it than its adequacy as a theory of individual human behaviour. So they surrendered any interest in the project of explaining individual behaviour. They insisted rather that RCT was a powerful tool for explaining and predicting the behaviour of markets, industries, economies. This brings us to John Maynard Keynes.

3. Keynes' Problem of Long Run Equilibrium

Lord Keynes famously said, 'In the long run we are all dead.' The full quote is worth reproducing: 'The long run is a misleading guide to current affairs. In the long run we are all dead. Economists set themselves too easy, too useless a task if in tempestuous seasons they can only tell us that when the storm is past the ocean is flat again.' [1923, Ch. 3.] The line is probably his most famous in a life of *bon mots*. Keynes' point was that a theory that could enable us to predict only long-run outcomes was of little use, even if it was correct. One could go further and argue, with Popper and Soros, that there is no way to tell if such a theory is correct and so it is not really a scientifically respectable theory at all.

Adam Smith first hypothesised that Rat Choice would, via the invisible hand, exploit self seeking to produce an outcome that would make every one better off. Economists sought to convert Smith's hypothesis into a mathematical theorem for the next 150 years. They succeeded, but at great cost.

Several factors conspired with Smith's insight to drive RCT to an unshakeable commitment to the existence, uniqueness and stability of a market clearing general equilibrium. To begin with, the tools of differential calculus that Walras and other 19th century economists shared with physics (and later also evolutionary biology) made it natural to search for equilibrium solutions to sets of simultaneous equations. More important was the evident fact of price stability – change one price and the result is not a market spiralling out of control, but what looks like a smooth readjustment. Over-generalise and the result is that one sees equilibrium everywhere

Equilibrium outcomes, if we can get them, provide several things economists want: first, like all social scientists, economists seek explanatory regularities in the chaotic swirl of human affairs. If underneath the booming, buzzing confusion, there are equilibria among significant social forces, then there are generalisations about them that we can discover: to start with, the laws of supply and demand. If there are no equilibria, the prospect of uncovering laws governing human affairs is much reduced. Second, the equilibrium outcomes of the interaction of rational choosers are probably allocatively efficient – they direct inputs to their optimal use in meeting the real, attainable wants of economic agents. As such, equilibrium analysis provides guidance to policy – public and private – about how to arrange matters to attain the beneficent outcome Smith's invisible hand hypothesis envisions. Of course, the fact that the equilibrium is unique and stable means that usually nothing need be done by government to attain it. *Laissez-faire*: left to itself the economy will get there.

As noted, because of their attraction to equilibrium analysis, economists spent about 150 years trying to make a mathematical theorem out of Smith's metaphor of the invisible hand making us all better off through the self seeking of each of us. They succeeded and congratulated themselves by awarding one of their earliest Nobel Prize to the economists who did it (Arrow and Debreu, 1954). What they proved was a weaker result than they wanted, but it was the best Rat Choice could do: In a perfectly competitive market of rational agents, the prices of all goods and services will arrive at a unique stable 'general' equilibrium that is allocatively (Pareto-) efficient. But the cost of providing the proof was draconian: the existence of the unique stable allocatively efficient equilibrium required so many false and impossible assumptions (five of them) besides those of RCT that the proof mainly explains why *actual* economic outcomes are neither welfare maximising nor allocatively efficient.

Observation suggests strongly that human affairs are rarely in equilibrium. At most patterns in human affairs are very local, temporary equilibria – broken up annually, monthly, daily, indeed sometimes hourly. Rat Choice theorists bid us to disregard or deprecate this inconvenient fact. Most changes, they argue, are temporary stochastic departures from the unique stable long-term equilibrium they have proved to exist. These temporary departures are fated to be cancelled out by equally random movements back towards the unique stable equilibrium.

It's rationality of the sort RCT asserts to be widespread that assures us of the existence of this happy outcome. Rational agents choose under conditions not of certainty, but of risk. Risk is the condition under which agents can assign probabilities to all alternative outcomes in accordance with three relatively weak axioms of probability theory. It's a direct implication of RCT that agents optimally allocate resources to the search for information they need. Recall the regress problem of Winter and Elster. An equally obvious implication of RCT is that they employ this information optimally to maximise their expected utility. If agents obey the laws of probability, new information is always incorporated into their expectations in accordance with Bayes' theorem. Two startling implications follow from these assumptions: first, under these circumstances, in the long run, everyone's probability assignments will converge on the same subjective probability assignments to all alternatives no matter where they start out. Second, because the errors people make are randomly distributed on a bell-shaped curve, the average value of their probability judgments will always be close to the objective (i.e. correct, actual) probabilities. Every individual's expectations may be wrong all the time, but the aggregate average of these wrong expectations will be the right expectation. Thus, in the long run, the market's expectations about outcomes are always correct. This is the basis of the continued confidence that markets really are allocatively efficient because they are informationally efficient – the efficient markets hypothesis.

Keynes' famous epithet reflects several criticisms of economics' attachment to equilibrium. Most have taken 'In the long run we are all dead' to mean that *laissez-faire* solutions to economic problems arrive too late to help the people who need it, if they arrive at all. But Keynes famously argued that instead of one unique, stable market clearing, allocatively efficient, equilibrium, there are many local equilibria which are far from allocatively efficient, and that governments can actually move economies out of these local equilibria in the short and medium run. Finally, and most subversively, he gave a reason to think that economies are never really on the move towards the long-run equilibrium of which the rational choice theorist dreams. The reason he gave was that humans often cannot act in accordance with the requirements of RCT. This fact deprives economics even of a theoretical assurance of the existence of an equilibrium that observation never detects.

The heart of Keynes' critique of mainstream equilibrium thought was his diagnosis of what RCT gets wrong and why. The diagnosis was perhaps not completely original with Keynes (Frank Knight (1921) prefigured Keynes and George Soros (2003) came at the same point, perhaps independently). It begins with a distinction between risk and uncertainty and explains the crucial role of money in the economy. Agents face conditions of risk if the alternatives facing them can be assigned probabilities that behave in accordance with the three axioms of probability theory, and which they can update in accordance with Bayes' theorem. Agents face conditions of uncertainty when it is impossible to assign probabilities to alternatives in this way.

Equilibrium economics is predicated on two assumptions: that risk is the rule and uncertainty the exception, and that probabilistic expectations of agents are distributed normally around the objective probabilities of events, cancelling out individual errors and making markets allocatively efficient. For this reason, *there is no room in mainstream economic theory for the existence of money*, a remarkable fact on which most microeconomists are silent.

In fact, humans generally face uncertainty, not risk. The difference between risk and uncertainty is the difference between the casino – in which all probabilities can be calculated, and living on an earthquake fault-line where no one has the slightest idea when the big one will hit. Exogenous – outside – events, big and small, intervene in almost all social processes almost all of the time. Agents don't, can't probabilify these events. Even if there are equilibria around which outcomes are moving, these exogenous events destroy them, substitute others, and destroy them too, in a continual process. It is a process that another great opponent of equilibrium thinking, Schumpeter (1942), called 'creative destruction,' though he should also have recognised the process of 'destructive destruction.' In the end, it's this continual destruction of general equilibrium trajectories before they reach their end points, that Keynes's pithy observation draws our attention to.

Uncertainty was the key to Keynes explanation of why money exists and what its real role in an economy is. The prevalence of uncertainty is one reason humans employ cognitive heuristics in decision making, instead of the RCT tools suited only to quantifiable risk. Uncertainty, and the way humans deal with it, produces multiple stable and unstable local equilibria, none of which are allocatively efficient, and all of which obstruct the economy's march to the mainstream economists' nirvana: general equilibrium.

So, social scientists', especially economists', commitment to equilibria is equal parts: wishful thinking about the invisible hand, attraction to mathematical elegance and tractability, and overconfidence in the rationality of human beings. It's a recipe for retrospective rationalisation and prospective impotence. There are, however, many *local* equilibria, some relatively long lasting. The existence of money is one such, and it raises another fundamental problem for RCT.

4. Hayek's Problem of 'Spontaneous Order'

It's not just that Rat Choice does not explain several of the important features of human life. *It cannot do so*. This Nobel Prize winning insight is due to an economist revered by many mainstream (i.e. Chicago-school) economists, Friedrich Hayek.[24] Here are three examples, all from economics, where you would assume rational choice has an explanatory role: the firm, money, and the price-system. Each of these institutions fulfils an important *need* individuals have. None emerged from a rational choice process. Hayek's problem was to figure out how they could have emerged and why they persist. He called them cases of 'spontaneous' emergence, persistence or order. But that is just to label the problem, as we'll see.

In the case of the firm, the human need is to solve the transaction-cost problem, as Ronald Coase (1937) first noticed. Without a solution to this problem, the division of labour must come to a standstill and with it almost all the productivity increases humans have contrived since the Middle Ages. No rational agent recognised what the problem

---

[24] Hayek's insight about the problem of spontaneous order and its explanatory solution did not of course prevent him from embracing RCT as an account of individual economic choice. His commitment to RCT of course endeared him to his colleagues at the University of Chicago, the epicentre of such commitments. Following Hayek some Chicago economists early invoked Darwinian processes to explain how rational choice is imposed on individual choice and eventuates by aggregation into unintended spontaneous but efficient outcomes such as the market. More lately Chicago economists have substituted rational expectations and representative rational agents operating in the market to effect efficient market outcomes, while foregoing any account of how markets could have arisen to begin with.

everyone faced was. No one decided to invent the firm in order to solve this problem. It emerged 'spontaneously' to 'order' exchanges between individuals that faced a transaction-cost problem. The firm is an example of 'spontaneous order.'

Money solves the biggest problem of barter: what the economists call 'double coincidence of wants'. Without money, if I want oranges and have only banana, I need to find someone who wants bananas and has oranges. What's more, if we can't divide and store bananas and oranges, I'll need to find someone who wants to trade in exact whole numbers of bananas and oranges that match up with the amounts I am prepared to trade. This is a problem that becomes intractable very early in human exchange. How does it get solved? Several times in distant cultures the same solution was hit upon: the emergence of a commodity with common features: portability, divisibility, durability, utility or widespread desirability, and short-term limits on its quantity. When money emerged no one around consciously recognised that money would have to have these features. (Something Hayek (1978) also noted.) No one rationally adopted some commodity in order to solve the problem of the double coincidence of wants. Rat Choice can't explain how it happened

The emergence of money requires that agents solve another problem: one of coordination. Sooner or later they must all converge on the same commodity. People must solve a 'common knowledge' problem. Somehow each agent must be willing to adopt a certain commodity as money, and must come to believe that everyone else will adopt the same commodity, and must believe that everyone else will be confident that every other agent has adopted the same commodity. You can see that this is a set of problems that can't be solved by individual rational choice, that were not solved by some explicit social contract. The institution of money is another example of order emerging without anyone intending it, or taking steps to bring it about. Of course to say money emerged spontaneously is simply to label the problem and exclude an obvious Rat Choice explanation of how it emerged.

The third example, Hayek's (1945) example, the system of market prices, is the most important – but the most difficult to understand – of these problems of spontaneous order. It was this realisation that earned Hayek his renown among economists.

The unsolvable problem of socialist central planning is informational. Central planning faces the mathematical problem of converting a list of available inputs and a list of desired outputs into a list of production orders, and then continually updating this list as input availability changes and desired outputs change. Central planning faces the further problem of sending information about each of the changes in inputs and outputs, only to those who need to have this information, in order to change their production plans. The central planner can't send the changes to everyone: we'd have to spend the better part of every day just trying to find the information we would need from a daily massive data dump. But the central planner can no more figure out to whom exactly to send the updated information than it can figure out the initial production order. These are all what mathematicians call NP-hard problems ('nondeterministic polynomial-time hard problems'). There is no known algorithmic, computerisable solution to such problems, and a good chance than none exists. Yet the problems are all solved all day and every day, instantaneously, by the system of market prices. The market price system is an information storage, retrieval and calculation system – a vast virtual computer – that provides the closest approximation to mathematically correct solutions to the central planners' calculation problems and at no cost whatever.

The market price system performs a function indispensable – not just to modern life – but to all human life beyond the Pleistocene. It is a function meeting a need that cannot have been foreseen by humans, no matter how rational; it is a solution to that need that no human or coalition of humans could have intentionally contrived. Indeed, it is a solution that rational choice would have led individuals to try to undermine or subvert in their own interests. It is a solution to the problem people face that is so ingenious it automatically and successfully responds to such subversion attempts.

The market price system operates continually to meet a need that no human or set of humans could, by intentional and deliberate action, fulfil, no matter how rational they are, and no matter how powerful and expensive their information storage, retrieval and computational resources are. And the market price system emerged, like money, spontaneously, independently, repeatedly and without malice of human forethought, throughout human affairs, across the globe.[25]

These three examples of spontaneous order highlight the economist's version of a problem facing all social sciences, a problem Rat Choice is incapable of dealing with. The problem is deep, and pervasive.

First, why pervasive? Because the three cases identified here are just the tip of an iceberg. Almost every phenomenon of interest to the social scientist manifests the problem of spontaneous order. Almost every human institution, almost every long-standing social practice, almost every organisation of individuals, and of their coalitions, fulfils a function, solves a problem, confers a benefit or advantage on something or other. Think of any of the variables of macroeconomics: the interest rate, the rate of inflation, the money supply, the fiscal deficit. These are institutions, or the properties of institutions with functions.

Unbeknownst to the agents who participate in them, the macroeconomic institutions fulfil important functions for the economy, for industries, for markets, and for

---

[25] There are of course domains, in which rational calculation is required to design 'incentive compatible' institutions, for example electronic bandwidth auctions in which there are a small number of bidders and strong pay-offs to collusion. Designing such institutions requires designers assume individuals are rational egoists and organise the institutions to defend themselves against undermining by such egoists.

their individual participants. Most of these functions are unrecognised, unintended and unforeseen most of the time, by most of their participants. But the functions fulfilled by these institutions are crucial to their emergence, persistence, change over time, and to their eventual disappearance. In this respect economic institutions are no different from almost all the political, social, cultural institutions, organisations, and practices that order the behaviour of individuals and groups. That means all social sciences face the problem of spontaneous order, not just economics. No social institution, organisation or practice could exist long enough even to be noticed by social scientists unless it had a function. Since most of the functions of most of the institutions that make human affairs possible go unnoticed, as well as unintended and undesigned by their participants, they all raise the problem of spontaneous order that Hayek noticed and that confronts the economist.

Almost everything of interest to the social scientist has a function, usually unintended and unforeseen and continually unrecognised. This observation was recognised, dimly and imperfectly, by functionalist social scientists, like Durkheim (1895) and Parsons (1951), in the first half of the 20th century. They recognised that most functions of most institutions escape the notice of their participants. These they called 'latent' functions, by contrast with the 'manifest' functions recognised and often designed, intended, and sustained by conscious deliberation and perhaps even by something approaching rational choice. The written US Constitution has manifest functions, some of them quite different from those of the unwritten British constitution. The former fulfils important latent functions not intended and not widely recognised. One reason British people are in certain respects – e.g. health care – far better off than American people is because the British constitution fills latent functions the US constitutions does not.

The 20th century functionalists were right about the functional character of almost all social institutions. But a serious oversight in their analysis condemned it to implausibility, and it went into eclipse long ago. The simple error functionalists made, which made their view sound so implausible, was to mis-identify the *beneficiaries* of the functions that institutions, practices, and organisations fulfilled. They assumed, quite myopically and wrongly, that the function of institutions, practices, organisations, was to fulfil the needs of people, of human beings. But it was obvious that many institutions, practices, organisations are in fact are harmful to people, confer no net advantage on them, for instance most religions, or Chinese foot-binding, or tobacco smoking. This Panglossianism about all social institutions made functionalism a laughing stock when it was not pilloried as an invitation to complacence and conservatism: if almost all human institutions fulfilled functions for us, then it is tempting to reason that we should not change them lest we deprive ourselves of the benefits they confer on us. Whence the charge of complaisance.

Only in the late 20th century did it become apparent that in these and other cases, a change in perspective – a *Gestalt switch* – would enable us to see what was not previously apparent: the relevant beneficiary of those features of institutions, practices, organisations harmful to people were the institutions, practices, organisational structures themselves, that parasitise people, that treat people as niches, environments to be exploited. Think of people as the environment and think of types of institutions, practices and organisations as the things that survive, replicate, and spread or recede and become extinct owing to the degree their features *exploit* human characteristics. Then the functionalist perspective becomes irresistible: many socially significant institutions, practices, organisations, confer huge net benefits on people – money, the firm, the market price system. Many others confer huge net harms on people, but in so doing ensure their own persistence – think again of foot binding or tobacco smoking or heroin addiction. Other institutions confer benefits on some people, and harms on others – slavery for example. Most institutions – religions, for example – confer a mixture of harms and benefits on different mixtures of persons over time.

One way to effect the gestalt switch necessary to accept thorough-going functionalism about human affairs is to employ the game theorist's notion of a 'strategy'. A 'strategy' is simply a rule, norm, procedure, of the form 'Under condition X, do Y'. Strategies may be reflexive or voluntary, moral, or ritual, matters of fashion or style, short-lived or not, obligatory or optional, complex or simple, consciously followed or not, beneficial to the agent employing them or harmful to him or her. People's behaviours are determined by strategies they internalise. These strategies are traits, like left-handedness, or speaking French, or wearing miniskirts, that can come and go. They are acquired, by social learning, by imitation, by unconscious classical and operant conditioning, and transmitted from person to person, and they interact with other strategies, cooperating with them, competing with them, subordinated to them, or subordinating them. Human social institutions, from a book club to Feudalism, are nested sets of coordinated strategies. Think of practices like patrilateral cross cousin marriage or purdah or the incest taboo. Think of organisations like the free masons or the parish council. 'Human affairs' is a matter of nested institutions, organisations, practices, all composed of the strategies individuals employ. Then there are the strategies each individual employs to navigate through these institutions, organisations, practices. The institutions, organisations, practices have functions. They thrive or perish depending on how well the strategies they impose on people enable the institutions, organisations and practices to fulfil these functions for their beneficiaries – often themselves.

To repeat: almost everything of interest to social scientists has a function, fulfils a need, confers a benefit, or is the direct consequence of something with a function. The pervasiveness of this feature of human affairs makes Hayek's problem of spontaneous order much more serious than even he supposed. Recall that problem: how do cases of spontaneous order emerge and persist? Rat Choice is not an option here. The institutions, practices, organisations that mainly interest us in social science have functions, attain ends, goals, confer advantages. Yet almost none of them were designed by men or gods. Hayek's achievement was to show that the economically most important of them *could not* have been the intended, designed or foreseen result of intentional action by rational agents. The problem of spontaneous order is: where did all these apparently well designed (but not actually designed at all) institutions, practices and organisations come from and why do they persist?

Hayek had the answer.

5. From Hayek to Soros, via Darwin

Wherever the appearance of design is to be met with, in nature or nurture, in the biological realm or the social realm, on the watchmaker's work bench or nature's laboratory, the source is never real foresight, but always tinkering – blind variation and environmental filtration. This is a lesson already well established in biology. But it is equally in force for the social and behavioural sciences. The lesson is resisted only because of the same mistake that obstructed the functionalist social scientists, combined with an equally egregious error of supposing that Darwinian processes are restricted to the domain of genetically hard-wired functions.

Every significant (unintended) feature of social life that has a function (and they almost all do) has been built by a Darwinian process. Why? Because there is no other alternative. Long ago, science – especially physical science – excluded the possibility of real goals, ends, purposes in nature. It revealed that future states couldn't reach back into the past and pull events in its direction. The Aristotelian conception that purposes explain anything at all has been progressively read out of every scientific domain until it is left only in folk psychology and its Rat Choice formalisation. (The idea is that correct expectations about the future, together with attainable desires about the future produce achieved futures. These futures are therefore part of the explanation of the processes that bring them about.) Purpose is hard for *hoi polloi* to shake. Part of the grip of RCT trades on its formalisation of common sense purposive explanation.

It was another 200 years after physics expunged purpose from its domain, before it was banished from the biological realm. Until 1859 the hand of the benevolent, omnipotent designer, God, was the favoured – indeed the only – explanation of the appearance of design in the domain of living things. This, in effect, made biology incompatible with physics and chemistry, sciences that had no need for the deity. The solution to the inconsistency was Darwin's discovery of the purely natural causal process that produces the appearance of design while showing that the appearance is not a reality. He showed biology had no more need of a deity than physics. There are no purposes at work in the biological realm. All biological functions are just adaptations produced by blind variation and passive environmental filtration.

There is no underestimating how powerful this result was – and remains – for reordering all the nonphysical sciences. It reconciles them with the most fundamental facts about nature physics discovered – that there are no purposes, goals, ends, designs out there waiting to be realised and playing a role in bringing about their realisers. Once Darwin showed how purely causal processes *could* bring about the appearance of design, biologists set about showing exactly how causal processes *did* bring them about: a 150 years of this work produced genetics and the molecular biology of the gene, protein, enzyme, neuron. It made thoroughly mechanical reproduction, respiration, development, and cognition.

If social processes, and all the interesting aspects of human affairs fulfil functions – for us, for themselves, for something else – if they show the appearance of having been designed to deliver some benefit to something or other, then they have to be the product of a Darwinian process of blind variation and passive environmental filtration. Why? Because that is the only way things with functions, adapted traits, can come about.[26]

Recall the suggestion above that we need to treat human institutions, groups, practices as packages of strategies employed by people. The features, characteristics, traits of institutions, organisations, practices, are composed of these packages of strategies. At the basement level of individual agents, the strategies they employ are their own individual adaptations – traits that have pay-offs for them or for someone else that result in these strategies persisting – being used over and over, and spreading – by imitation or instruction, reinforcement or coercion, or receding by operant punishment, or legal sanction, etc. Individual strategies are traits of individual people. Their cognitive equipment is what passes them on, modifies them. The human environment, including all the nested packages of strategies that constitute institutions, organisations and practices, select among these strategies in ways that result in the emergence, persistence, and change – rapid and slow – of individual strategies, and nested groups of them.

Here game theory (the scientific study of strategic interactions) is a pedagogic help. Types of games are characterised by pay-offs and strategies available to be played. In the prisoner's dilemma, one can cooperate or defect. The rational strategy is to defect. Bigger institutions, practices, organisations are composed of strategies played by their smaller component institutions, practices and organisations, and in the end, by the

---

[26] At this late date it may not bear mentioning that there is no commitment to secular 'progress,' continual improvement, or some biological, social or moral betterment of later evolutionary outcomes over earlier ones. Darwin's insight was that all adaptation is local, that today's adaptation in the current environment will be tomorrow's maladaptation in a different environment, and that there is absolutely nothing morally better or improving about increased fitness. Sen (2002) effectively criticizes mistaken conceptions about Darwinian progress. But neither Darwin nor latter-day exponents of Darwinian cultural evolution make any such commitments.

individual participants, people, whose interaction produces these larger social units and their features, as the unintended, unforeseen result of their individual strategies. (Students of the philosophy of social science will recognise this claim as the thesis of methodological individualism, a thesis familiar to economists and Popperians.)

Given the pay-offs – costs and benefits – that institutions, practices, organisations impose on the use of various strategies, there is selection for those that do better, regardless of whether the people who play them recognise the pay-offs or are motived by them. Who decides on the pay-offs to various strategies? Almost always no individual does. It's nature that decides in the earliest, simplest institutions. For example, the strategies of males and females in the hunter-gatherer domestic division of labour, were selected for by their impact on off-spring survival. As institutions, practices, and organisations emerge, they increasingly set the pay-offs to participating strategies, to other strategies that may undermine or unravel them, and to strategies that compete with them. Of course institutions, practices, roles, spawn new institutions, groups, and practices, often by combining into larger units with new functions, and also by selecting for smaller component units, cooperative ones, and exploitative ones.

In biological adaptation by natural selection there is a well-understood process that operates through adaptation to produce both increasing complexity and diversity. The same forces operate in human affairs. The persistent processes of random variation and passive filtration produce complex and diverse social institutions, practices and organisations – ones with new adaptations, new functions.

Think about strategies that people employ as the traits out of which the traits of all the rest of social processes are composed. Think about these strategies and packages of them that constitute institutions, as having traits that enable them to colonise humans, to spread, to compete, to cooperate, to synergise and support, or subvert and exploit one another.

Hayek realised that this Darwinian approach to the domain of the social sciences is not merely a useful metaphor, a suggestive trope, a way of looking at things we had not noticed before. There are two reasons a Darwinian cultural mechanism is an unavoidable reality in human affairs, and therefore an indispensable tool for understanding them.

First, as noted above, a Darwinian approach to human affairs is 'the only game in town'. We know, with great confidence, that there is only one way that functions, adaptations – the appearance of purpose or design, can emerge in a world like ours: the way Darwin discovered. Unless we are prepared to deny that social institutions, practices, organisations, have functions, we are stuck having to apply Darwin's discovery to human affairs. Applying the Darwinian approach requires a lot of work. We cannot expect to simply apply the details of how Darwinian selection works in biology to human affairs. Darwinian cultural processes will not employ the mechanisms (especially the genetic ones) Darwinian biological processes do. The Darwinian approach to human affairs does not require genetic determinism of human differences, the innateness of important human traits, the hard-wiring of human culture, or an evolutionary psychology about human cognitive and emotional traits. Blind variation and passive environmental filtering are as much matters of culture as matters of nature.

Second, and for present purposes more important, recognising the Darwinian character of all processes in the domain of the social sciences helps solve the three problems that daunt RCT: the problem of rational fools; the problem that by the time equilibrium arrives we are all dead; and the mystery of spontaneous order. And it does all these three things in a way that vindicates an important insight George Soros has been articulating in lectures, papers and books for about 30 years.

Sen's problem of rational fools is that rational agents won't provide themselves with the fruits of cooperation since cooperation is just a set of strategies that the rational agent can free ride upon. Even when cooperation is a Nash equilibrium strategy, the rational agent will continually seek opportunities to change the pay-offs, take advantages, free-ride, secure rents. Enduring cooperation robust enough to withstand threats requires commitment, usually driven by emotions, that override rational choice. This is the lesson of much of the research on the evolution of cooperation: research that explicitly employs Darwinian dynamics – mechanisms of random variation and natural selection to identify strategies that maximise fitness. These strategies are rarely ones RCT recommends.

Besides Sen's rational fools problem there is the calculation/implementation problem that faces RCT. Besides the regress in applying it to decide how much to invest in acquiring information, the absence of risk/presence of uncertainty in choice, make Rat Choice often maladaptive as a real-world decision strategy. What we employ instead are heuristics – rules of thumb and rules of thought that provide quick and dirty solutions to real-time problems. Our hardwired cognitive strategies are the ones natural selection found through geological eons of tinkering. Our learned cognitive strategies are ones Darwinian cultural selection has produced by trial and error and transmitted by teaching. In Herbert Simon's (1955) terms, humans don't optimise, they satisfice, just as Darwinian natural selection – the satisficing process *par excellence* – would have them do.

Darwinian cultural selection enables us to fully understand both spontaneous order and the real role of equilibria in human affairs. Once we see how it does these two things we will be in a position to appreciate Soros' conception of reflexivity and how pervasively it influences all aspects of human affairs.

Turn for a moment to Darwinian processes in the biological realm. Here there is a considerable role for equilibrium analysis and it is an important tool in both the mathematical modelling of biological processes and in the explanation of biological regularities or laws.

An illustration will help greatly. It is a regularity that in almost all vertebrate species, indeed in almost all sexually reproducing species, the sex ratio is 1:1 – 50 %

males, 50 % females. That there is almost always, almost exactly the same number of men as women, was long treated as strong evidence of the benevolence of God. The 20th century British geneticist, R.A. Fisher, showed that the 1:1 sex ratio generalisation is a stable equilibrium which results from a Darwinian process of blind variation and passive environmental filtration. Women have varying hereditary predispositions to give birth to males or to females. Whenever the sex ratio departs from 1:1 in favour of more females, those mothers who disproportionately bare male children will have more and fitter grandchildren, since their sons are scarcer relative to females and can be choosier. More grandchildren carrying genes that favour having boys results in more boys and so moves the sex ratio back to 1:1. When ratio begins to favour males over females the same process in reverse shifts it back to 50% of each. Whence the stable equilibrium and the biological law that sex ratios remain the same and in balance.

Actually it's not a law, because it is false for a small number of species. In humans the long run equilibrium sex ratio at birth is 1.05 to 1, slightly favouring male births. Why? Because boys' mortality rates are higher than girls', or at least were higher in the environment that selected for homo sapiens. Darwinian natural selection had to fine tune the sex ratio to make it 1:1 at sexual maturity. Doing that required more boys at birth than girls. Additionally, there are several species of insects in which the sex ratio is heavily biased towards females.

How does the fine-tuning on the one hand, and the cases of complete abrogation of the apparent biological law on the other, happen? There are many examples of fine-tuned equilibria in the biological realm. The Fisher sex ratio is but one very easily understood example. Any two traits of organisms that work together well, such as flying and good eye-sight in birds, or symbiotic traits – cleaner fish and cleaned shark, remain in equilibrium for a long time once established. Competing traits do so as well: think of predator and prey species that maintain a long term relationship, neither becoming too rare or too numerous to make the other extinct. And of course the traits of parasites and hosts show the same process of fitness maximising equilibration over time: a parasite so virulent that it kills a host before it can jump to the next host becomes extinct, leaving the less virulent form to spread, and so it goes until parasite and host can just live with each other, as in the Simian version of the AIDS HIV.

These are all cases of 'local equilibrium'. But underneath the appearance of changelessness, balance, calm stasis in the fixed relationship between traits, there is an underground guerilla war taking place. Each population of traits among cooperative ones or competing ones, in the same species or in different interacting ones, is in constant variation – random mutation. Almost all of these mutations are, of course, unfavourable in their local environments – the combination of the competing or cooperating trait and the rest of the niche in which the mutation finds itself. Very rarely, one of these random variants confers an advantage to a trait and the organism that bears it. The new trait enables the organism to exploit its hitherto cooperating partner, or to suddenly achieve an advantage over its hitherto equally fit competitor. At this point, the local equilibrium begins to break up. The only thing that can prevent it from eventually unravelling completely is a counter-variation in the traits that hitherto cooperated or competed effectively enough: a counter-variation fit enough to preserve the equilibrium. For obvious reasons, the process that ensues when local equilibria break up, are called *arms races*.

The natural history of the planet is a history of local equilibria broken up and followed by arms races in the biological domain. The local equilibria are imposed by natural selection operating through very small variations over enormous time scales in very slowly changing environments. They produce regularities that short-lived creatures might mistake for fixed laws of nature: giraffes have long necks, polar bears are white, Australian mammals are marsupial. And when environments are constant for long enough some of the regularities reflect equilibria that approach fitness optima very closely, for example the 1.05 to 1 sex ratio in humans.

Sometimes these local equilibria last for only a brief time and are broken up quickly. The best examples of such rapid evolutionary change, where arms races are the rule and equilibria are the exceptions, is the evolution of bacterial drug resistance. The AIDS virus varies so rapidly, owing to instability of its RNA genome, that it can quickly defeat any single retroviral agent. For this reason the only effective treatment of AIDS requires the use of three different drugs in combination which reduces the probability of a variant arising to a low enough level to prevent resistance building up.

So, natural selection produces traits that are locally adapted, i.e. that perform functions, confer net benefits to whatever bears these traits. Natural selection packages these traits together into local equilibria that endure for varying time periods – hundreds of millions of years in some cases, depending on the constancy of the environment. But these equilibria are always liable to be ended when environments change or when persistent though blind variations that add or change traits in ways better able to exploit or even destroy the local equilibrium. Since environments change slowly, many local equilibria emerge and increasingly approach local optima. Therefore they resist undermining by random variations, and the resulting biological regularities usually endure for eons. But when environments begin to change rapidly, the geographic range and the life-times of local regularities begins to shorten. By the time you get to disease-causing bacteria and host, the local equilibria are very short lived.

The application of all this to human affairs is obvious, direct and highly significant. To begin with, it solves Hayek's problem. Spontaneous order is relatively long lasting and widespread local equilibrium. It is the result of Darwinian cultural selection operating on strategies, packaging them together in ways that pay off for participants – often cooperating or competing individuals, sometimes coalitions of them. Others of these strategies get packaged together into institutions that parasitise all their participants or only some, symbiotically benefiting others, or more likely doing both at the same time, to differing degrees, to all participants, practitioners, group members.

Consider the three examples from economics developed above: money, the firm, and the price system. We could have picked others, examples of political institutions – parliamentary democracy, social practices like the Indian caste system, complex cross-cousin marriage rules that anthropologists have uncovered, historically long-lived practices such as primogenitor, or the fashionability of an innovation, like the iPhone. Each of these reflects a local equilibrium, some very long lived such as the caste system, some not quite as old, such as parliamentary democracy, others fleeting reflections of Schumpeter's creative destruction. Our three very long lived examples – the firm, money, and the price system have been around, and will continue to be, owing to the importance of the functions they fulfil, and the low probability of environmental change or variants emerging that could unravel them. Over the eons, people have consciously and unconsciously adopted strategies that attempt to take advantage of each of them – rent seeking – by counterfeiting, or currency debasement in the case of money, by a range of business frauds in the case of the firm, by market cornering, or price controls, or insider trading in the case of the price system.

In each case the institution has responded, through new variations in the strategies that compose it, in ways that successfully resisted subversion. The local equilibrium each of them constitutes has persisted, as the institutions have found ways to adapt to changes in their environments. Institutions like money, the firm, the price system last long enough to provide an environment, a framework within which many more local, more short-lived equilibria come and go. These more local equilibria emerge as individual environmental adaptations, and co-adaptations, temporarily well matched competitors, or combinations of them. The environments within which these packages of strategies are co-adapted, are ones created by institutions and practices such as money, the firm, and the market price system. Keynes's long run equilibrium has arrived for a few long-lived fundamental human institutions. Local equilibria are nested within them, and the more local they are, the easier to break up, till at some level of strategic interaction, there are no local equilibria or none lasting long enough to exploit.

6. Sorosian Uncertainty and Reflexivity

The impermanence, instability, multiplicity and indeed the absence of equilibria in day-to-day, or even month-to-month human affairs brings us to Soros, and his insights. These insights do two things: most important, they give us the mechanism through which the Darwinian processes operate to make and break spontaneous orders. Less important, they vindicate Popper's thesis of the unity of science, the one doctrine of Sir Karl that Soros rejects.

Soros makes two two claims:

The human uncertainty principle: humans are fallible, in fact usually mistaken in their expectations, including their probabilistic ones. They predict inaccurately and these predictions cannot be improved, for example by honouring the principles of probability theory more fully.

Reflexivity: Agents' earlier expectations about future outcomes combine with their preferences in ways that change the future outcomes, often so greatly as to bear no resemblance to their earlier expectations and to fail to satisfy their preferences.

In *The Alchemy of Finance* Soros uses the combined, iterated, and cyclical operation of these two regularities to undermine the confidence economists have that we are ever near the 'long-run-all-dead' general equilibrium. He uses them to explain how several obvious facts absurdly denied by RCT-dominated economic theory in fact obtain – e.g. bubbles and busts. And Soros employs them to show that prediction is impossible – in financial markets in particular.

An example illustrates the uncertainty/reflexiveness process at its starkest, where it produces bubble and busts in the stock market. In thinking about the extreme cases it is important to keep in mind that the process operates everywhere, and produces *routine* changes as well as *non-routine* ones.

The graph is based on one in *The Alchemy of Finance*, p. 56. In brief, the red curve of stock prices reflects the strategies of agents – mutual funds, hedge funds, individuals, etc. This curve reflects the aggregate of agents' uncertain, unforesighted expectations about companies' futures. The blue line imperfectly reflects the business success of companies, i.e. the equally uncertain strategies and packages of strategies of CEOs, managers, sales reps, and the shop-floor workers, and consumers, who effect the companies actual earnings per share.

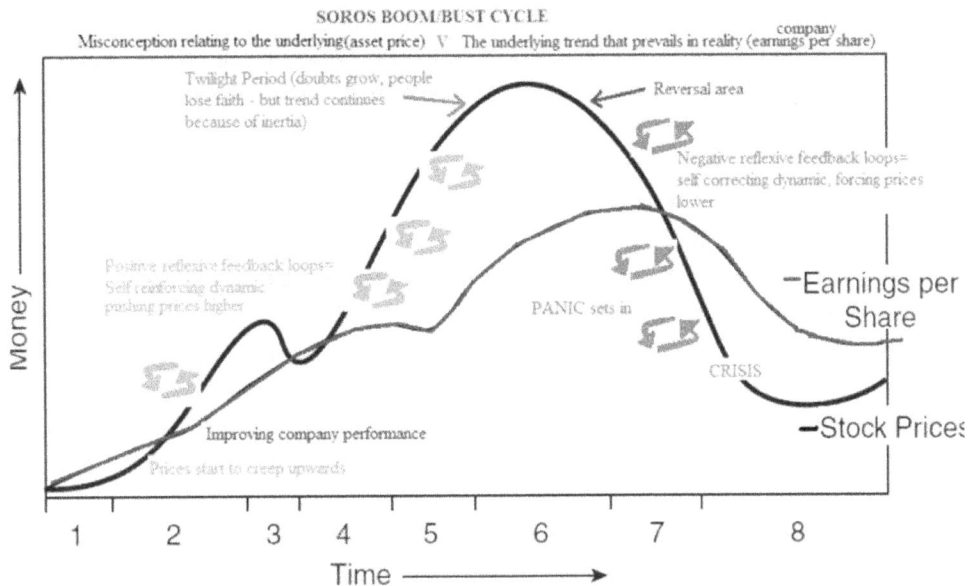

Figure 1. Stock prices track earnings and vice versa – i.e. reflexively.

Following Keynes and Knight, Soros insists that the scope for probability is extremely limited: errors do not fall on a bell-shaped curve around the truth, and new evidence does not drive it in that direction either. For that reason RCT's substitution of risk for certainty is not a significant improvement on the standard assumption of complete information. Equally important, in figure 1, the shapes of the two curves reflect the fact that earlier stock prices influence later earns per share, and vice versa. Peoples' (fallible) expectations about future states of affairs have effects on how those future states turn out, and these future states effect people's later (and always fallible) expectations. The combination of reflexivity and uncertainty, when not held in check, produce swings in two (or more) factors locked in a reflexive relation, and usually much wider swings on the expectations side of the relationship.

Expectations by themselves won't effect anything. They need to be acted upon. (Sometimes Soros calls this the 'manipulative' function of thinking, sometimes he calls it the 'participating' function.) So, reflexiveness is a relationship between strategies. But strategies are driven by expectations that lack foresight. They are almost always individually wrong, very often also wrong on average, and when the expectations are right and drive successful strategies, they are right by accident!

Now, the combination of strategy-uncertainty and strategy-reflexiveness does not simply produce wild swings in financial markets – bubbles and bubble-bursts. It operates everywhere in human affairs, because reflexivity is the rule and not the exception in these affairs. Strategies that one set of agents and organisations employ to exploit other peoples' and other organisations sets of strategies effect the second set of strategies and these in turn effect the success and thus the spread and persistence of the first set of strategies. This makes human affairs unpredictable to participants owing to the ineliminable combination of uncertainty and reflexivity that drives the choice of strategies reflexively linked.

Contrast the picture of Sorosian reflexivity/uncertainty with the mainstream economists' picture: Rat Choice economic theory would have these curves move very closely together, since all parties are hypothesised to employ probability theory and the average of their expectations cancel out to the actual objective probabilities. The two curves should move in lock-step. This is the efficient markets hypothesis, reflected in figure 2.

Fundamental Nominal Return Versus Market Nominal Return
Growth of $1: 1872 – 2001

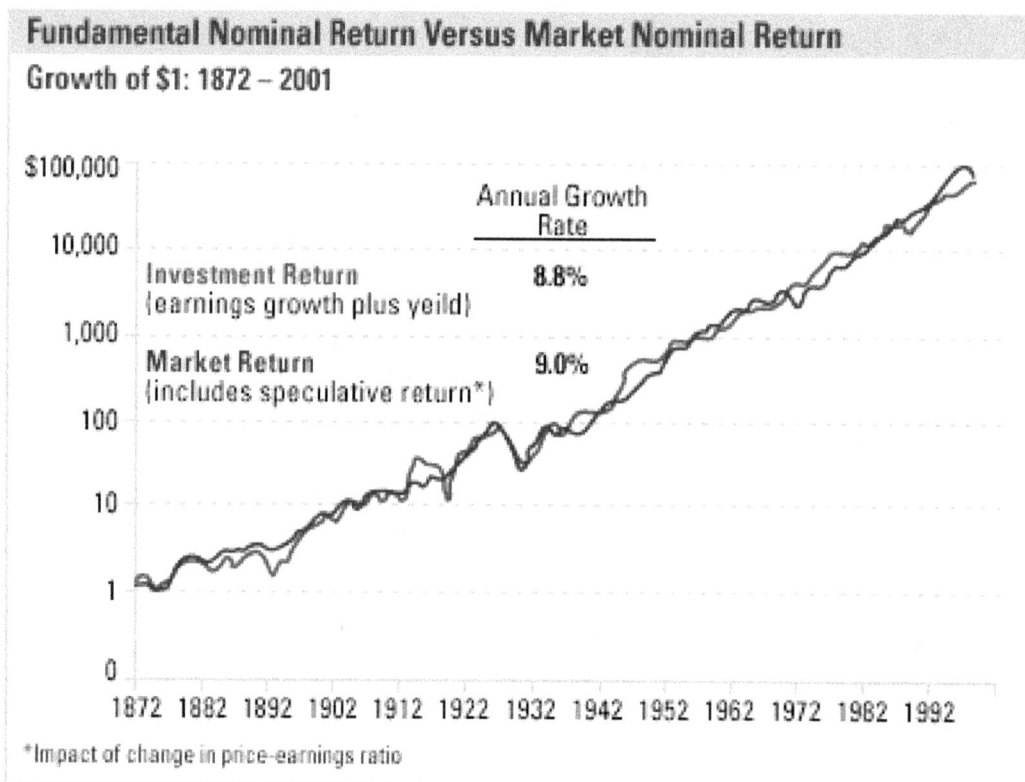

*Impact of change in price-earnings ratio

Figure 2. Stock prices track earnings over a 120 year period.

If Soros is correct the combination of reflexivity and uncertainty makes mainstream, general equilibrium-oriented, economics impossible.

How do we know Soros is correct and mainstream economics, Rat Choice and the microeconomic 'paradigm' they drive is wrong? Which graph above is correct, figure 1, the Soros boom/bust curve, or figure 2, the 120 years of efficient markets? The empirical data by themselves won't decide. There are many reasons they can't decide. But the main reason they can't is that a) it is equivocal, b) data collection is theoretically driven and doesn't point in the direction of any theory without a great deal of theoretical adjustment and interpretation. We know that Soros' insights about uncertainty in expectations and reflexivity in their effects are right because these two processes are driven by the Darwinian processes. The same Darwinian processes prevent us from being rational fools, make us users of fast and frugal heuristics, produce spontaneous order, and shape the institutions, groups and practices through which humans navigate. Sorosian reflexivity and uncertainty is a matter of Darwinian forces acting in human culture. Let's see exactly why.

The graph below represents a typical predator-prey population cycle over time. In this case, lynx and hare populations cycle between limits with a constant six-month lag between population maxima and population minima.

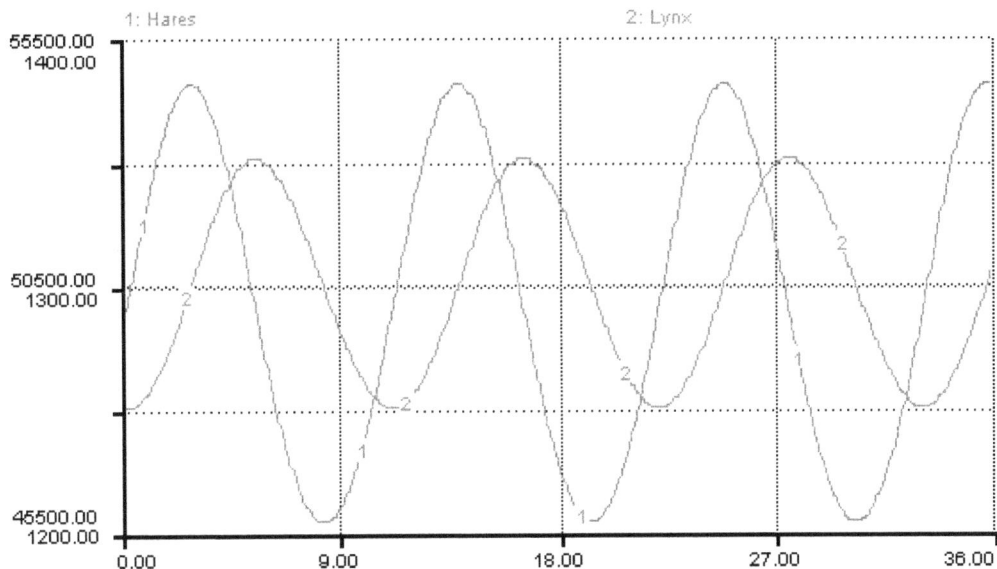

The cause of this pattern is a combination of reflexivity and uncertainty. Lynx survive by employing the strategy of preying on hare. Lynx-predatory strategies select for hare strategies that are good at avoiding lynx-predation. Successful hare hunting strategies increases lynx populations, but this reduces later hare populations and so even later reflexively reduces lynx populations by reducing the pay-offs to their predation strategies.

The reflexiveness of the relationship between lynx and hare strategies is well understood in evolutionary biology: each set of strategies is subject to linked frequency dependent selection with a lag. Each is maintained within a certain minimal and maximal range by stabilising selection. Underneath this stable cycle, both lynx and hares are varying their behaviours randomly, without foresight. Mother nature faces the same kind of uncertainty we humans face.

Now, compare this curve to the Soros boom/bust cycle curve. It's the same curve of lagged reflexiveness of stock prices to earnings per share, the same relationship between strategies of stock-pickers and strategies at work in firms reflected in their earnings per share. The difference is that the predator-prey graph covers four cycles, and Soros's covers just one.

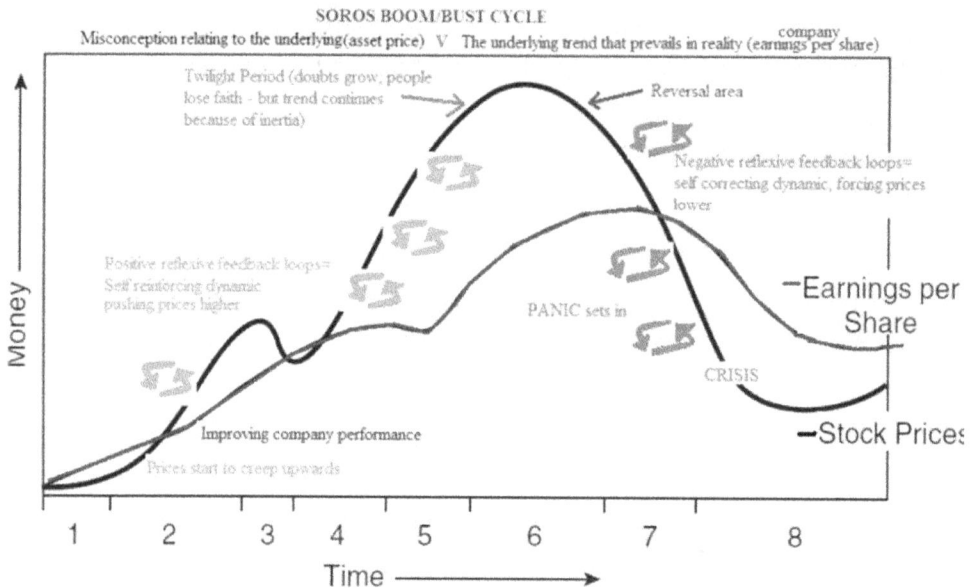

SOROS BOOM/BUST CYCLE

Misconception relating to the underlying (asset price) V The underlying trend that prevails in reality (earnings per share)   company

Twilight Period (doubts grow, people lose faith - but trend continues because of inertia)

Reversal area

Negative reflexive feedback loops= self correcting dynamic, forcing prices lower

Positive reflexive feedback loops= Self reinforcing dynamic pushing prices higher

PANIC sets in

—Earnings per Share

CRISIS

Improving company performance

Prices start to creep upwards

—Stock Prices

Money

Time

Figure 1. Again.

The point is not simply that the curves in each graph share the same relationship. The processes they describe are the same. And the Darwinian selective process that gives rise to them is the same too: reflexiveness and uncertainty. In biological contexts *reflexiveness* is the linked frequency-dependent selection of strategies that compete, cooperate, are parasitical or symbiotic. In the biological domain the *uncertainty*, the lack of foresight in strategy-choice, is reflected in their persistence coupled with the blindness of variations among them. Both operate in Darwinian cultural processes to produce the same phenomena.

The difference between the biological and the cultural is a difference of degree – the tempo and mode of evolution.

In the biological domain reflexivity and uncertainty are usually kept in bounds that produce stable cycles, ones that even vindicate some limited confidence in predictions among ecologists, agricultural scientists, even some epidemiologists. The two reasons are obvious. Reflexivity changes the environment. But it rarely changes the environment within which a strategy is played so much that it drives itself to extinction, or to complete dominance – fixation in the biologist's terminology. Extinctions are well understood. Fixations less so. About the only example of a strategy that in nature has achieved complete domination is the strategy of coding genetic information in nucleic acids. Somewhat less dominant, but almost universal, is the 1:1 ratio between strategies of bearing males vs. females within the 'environment' created by sexual reproduction (though we don't yet know what environmental 'design problem' selected for the strategy of sexual reproduction itself). The second constraint that keeps reflexive strategies cycling in balance is that the range of random variation is limited, the differences in pay-offs to the variants is small, and their rates of replication are slow, requiring a generation or so. All this means that some local equilibria in biology last long enough that it is worthwhile locating them and trying to exploit them in applied science.

In Darwinian cultural processes, none of these constrains operate, and they produce Sorosian phenomena everywhere. The rate at which strategies replicate (through imitation as well as instruction and enforcement) has been accelerating over the entire 50,000 years of human cultural evolution, and the range of variations in these strategies has also proliferated, though it is crucial to bear in mind that they are as lacking in foresight as ever. What is more, owing to the nested character of human institutions with functions, and the speed with which they change, there has been very strong selection for strategies that track changes in other strategies and influence them as well, that is, for reflexive strategies. Finally, environments change, and once human culture and its inevitable reflexivity crosses a threshold, most selective environments never remain stable long enough to allow for the *repetition* of the same boom/bust cycles that make them of any predictive use. The efficient markets curve above looks regular and reliable until you look at the time scale on the bottom of the curve. It's 130 years! Spread out the curve and it provides no guidance any one can use in day-to-day, week-to-week, month-to-month strategy selection!

In the biological domain, uncertainty and reflexivity are held in check by environments that change with geological slowness. This produces long-lived local equilibrium outcomes. In the human domain, the environment is cultural. It is composed of nested sets of strategies that are all affected by both reflexivity and uncertainty. The result of their operation is at most short-lived local equilibria, broken up by radical environmental change. The source of this radical environmental change in human cultural processes is obvious. It is the iterated, unsynchronised combinations of reflexivity and uncertainty in strategy variation. As the rate of change in the cultural environment increases, the lifetimes of local equilibria shorten, until in many cases they disappear altogether. Human affairs appear chaotic because many of them are far from equilibrium, even if there are any equilibria to which they may temporarily be heading.

The problem reflexivity makes for all human agents is that almost all local equilibria of interest to us are too short lived to be exploited. Owing to reflexivity, many equilibria last for an hour or a day or a week or a month. By the time people have noticed, and figured out how to exploit them, they have evanesced, disappeared, been broken up by a new variant that breaks them up and substitutes a new, equally short-lived equilibrium, or perhaps an arms race, rapidly searching through the 'space' of strategy-variations for a new impermanent equilibrium. When some innovation – a new fashion, gadget, political slogan – does manage to exploit a local equilibrium, we can be confident that it arose without foresight, and that it will probably disturb the local equilibrium immediately, eventually break it up completely, and then itself fall victim to some newer strategy.

There are of course many, very long-lasting, local equilibria in human affairs. Most of them persist owing to be benefits they accord people, some exist in spite of the net costs they impose on people. They can be exploited by policy design and implementation; some of them can even be unravelled by policy, for example, consider the fate of tobacco smoking in western society over the last half-century. Most long-lived, widespread local equilibria are hard for small numbers of individuals to exploit or undermine. It's the short-lived local equilibria that are the targets of 'rent-seeking' – in business especially. And they are too short lived for any simple recipe for securing such rents to succeed for long.

Acknowledgements

Thanks to John Latsis, Constantinos Repapis, Dorian Julien, audiences at the Central European University, Purdue University, the Philosophy of Social Science Roundtable at the University of California, Santa Cruz, and most of all George Soros, for comments on previous versions of this essay.

References

Arrow, K., Debreu, G. (1954) 'Existence of an Equilibrium for a Competitive Economy', *Econometrica*, 22, No. 3, pp. 265-290.

Buchanan, J. B. (1990) *The Economics and the Ethics of Constitutional Order* (Ann Arbor: University of Michigan Press).

Campbell, D. T., et. al. (1966) *Unobtrusive Measures: nonreactive research in the social sciences* (Chicago: Rand McNally).

Durkheim, E. (1995) *The Rules of the Sociological Method*, (New York: Free Press) 1982.

Edgworth, F. Y. (2003) *Mathematical psychics, and further papers on political economy* (Oxford University Press).

Elster, J. (1978) *Logic and Society* (New York: Cambridge University Press).

Frank, R. (1988) *Passion within Reason* (New York: W.W. Norton).

Gigerenzer, G. et. al., *Ecological Rationality* (New York: Oxford University Press).

Hayek, F. (1945) 'The Uses of Knowledge in Society,' *American Economic Review*. 35, No. 4. pp. 519-30.

Hayek, F. (1978) 'The Denationalization of Money', in Hayek, 1999, *Good Money* Part II (London: Routledge).

Jevons, W. S. (1877) *The Theory of Political Economy* (London: Macmillan).

Kahneman, D. (2003) 'A Psychological Perspective on Economics,' *American Economic Review*, 93, pp. 162-168.

Kahneman, D. (2011) *Thinking, Fast and Slow* (New York: Farrar, Straus and Giroux).

Keynes, J.M. (1923) *Tract on Monetary Reform* (London: MacMillan).

Keynes, J.M. (1937) *The General Theory of Employment, Interest and Money* (London: McMillan).

Knight, F. (1921) Risk, *Uncertainty and Profit* (New York: Houghton Mifflin).

Mackenzie, R. (1984) *Constitutional Economics* (Lexington: Mass).

Parsons, T. (1951) *The Social System*, London (Routledge: London).

Popper, K. (2004) *Conjectures and refutations: the growth of scientific knowledge* (London: Routledge).

Schumpeter, J. A. (1942) *Capitalism, Socialism and Democracy* (New York: Harper).

Sen, A. (1977) 'Rational Fools: A Critique of the Behavioral Foundations of Economic Theory,' *Philosophy & Public Affairs*, 6, (4) (Summer, 1977), pp. 317-344.

Sen, A. (1997) *Development as Freedom* (New York: Anchor Books).

Sen, A. (1993) 'On the Darwinian View of Progress,' *Population and Development Review*, 19, pp. 123-137.

Simon, H. (1955) 'A Behavioral Theory of rational choice,' *Quarterly Journal of Economics*, 69, pp. 99-188.

Soros, G. (2003) *Alchemy of Finance* (New York: Wiley).

Wicksteed, P.H. (1910) *The Common Sense of Political Economy* (London: Macmillan).

Winter, S. G. (1975) 'Optimization and Evolution in the theory of the firm,' *Adaptive Economic Models* (ed. By R.G. Day and T. Groves) (New York: Academic Press), pp. 73-118.

SUGGESTED CITATION:

Rosenberg, A. (2014) 'From Rational Choice to Reflexivity: Learning from Sen, Keynes, Hayek, Soros, and most of all, from Darwin'. *Economic Thought*, 3.1, pp. 21-41.
http://www.worldeconomicsassociation.org/files/journals/economicthought/WEA-ET-3-1-Rosenberg.pdf

Adam Smith's Natural Prices, the Gravitation Metaphor, and the Purposes of Nature

David Andrews, Department of Economics, State University of New York at Oswego, USA
david.andrews@oswego.edu

Abstract

Adam Smith's 'natural price' has long been interpreted as a 'normal price' or 'centre of gravitation price' based on the famous gravitation metaphor of the *Wealth of Nations* I.vii, natural in the sense that it is the price that would result if competition were truly free, unobstructed by monopoly or government regulation, and could also therefore be called normal price, appealing to a sense of natural opposed to that which is produced artificially.

This essay has three purposes. First I criticise this interpretation of Smith's gravitation metaphor. For Smith, it is not a Newtonian metaphor for the attractive character of natural price, but rather an Aristotelian metaphor for the pattern of movement of market prices, in which natural price serves merely as a reference point.

Second I present an interpretation of Smith's natural price based on his understanding of nature, in the context of his assertions that the goals of nature are the self-preservation of individuals and the propagation of species, goals humans pursue with divided labour under bonds of mutual dependence, facilitated by exchange and hence prices. The natural price of a commodity is the price that supports nature's goals by providing for the maintenance of those who participate in production and supply in a manner that is just sufficient for these activities to continue indefinitely.

Third I highlight the similarity between natural prices construed in this way and the prices of Piero Sraffa's *Production of Commodities by Means of Commodities*.

Keywords: Adam Smith, Piero Sraffa, natural price, normal price, nature, gravitation

Introduction

At least since Alfred and Mary Paley Marshall's *The Economics of Industry* (1879), Adam Smith's 'natural price' has been interpreted as a 'normal price' or 'centre of gravitation price' based on the famous gravitation metaphor of Chapter 7 of Book One of the *Wealth of Nations*: 'The Normal Price, or as Adam Smith says, "the natural price is as it were the central price to which the prices of all commodities are continually gravitating. Different accidents may sometimes keep them suspended a good deal above it, and sometimes force them down even somewhat below it. But whatever may be the obstacles which hinder them from settling in this center of repose and continuance, they are constantly tending towards it'" (Marshall and Marshall 1879, p. 77; citing Smith *WN* I.vii.15).

The Marshalls took the gravitation metaphor to mean that natural price is natural in the sense that it is the price that would result if competition were truly free, unobstructed by monopoly or government regulation, and could also therefore be called normal price, appealing to a sense of natural opposed to that which is produced artificially.

A similar interpretation has been adopted by a number of more recent writers on classical political economy who argue, along with Marshall, that the centre of gravitation mechanism plays a crucial role in Smith's theory of natural price, writers including Pierangelo Garegnani, Geoffrey Harcourt, Ian Steedman, John Eatwell, Murray Milgate, Tony Aspromourgos, Heinz Kurz and Neri Salvadori.

'As we all know, [theorists including Adam Smith] understood the long-period position as the "centre" towards which the competitive economy would gravitate in the given long-period conditions' (Garegnani 1976, p. 27).

'The classical authors did not consider the "normal" values of the variables as purely ideal or theoretical; they saw them rather as "centres of gravitation", or "attractors", of actual or market values' (Kurz and Salvadori 1998, p. 3).

'Natural prices are the competitive "centre of gravitation" for fluctuations of market (i.e. actual) prices. By creating these categories Smith defined what the theory of value, the core of any analysis of a market economy, was to be about' (Eatwell and Milgate 1999, p. 83).

'With regard to commodity prices, the centerpiece of Smith's approach is a dynamic process: the converging or "gravitating" of market prices toward natural prices via competition' (Aspromourgos 2010, pp. 65-6).

'Ever since the Physiocrats and Adam Smith, political economists have wrestled with the relationship between observable market prices [and] underlying natural prices ... Central to this analysis has been the concept of a centre of gravitation ... Common to them all is the concept of a central attractor' (Harcourt and Kriesler 2012, p. 9).[27]

Despite substantial differences regarding the theory of value, Marshall shares with these scholars the idea that Smith's natural price is to be understood in terms of the economic process Smith illustrated with the gravitation metaphor. On this shared understanding, natural price is natural first and foremost because it is the price which is the outcome toward which market prices tend to move if they are neither obstructed nor restrained: 'whatever the differences between the two kinds of theory [that of the classical writers and that of Marshall] ... what concerns us here is only to point out that the notion of "long-period positions" as "centres" of gravitation was fundamentally the same in the two cases' (Garegnani 1976, p. 29).

This essay has three purposes, the first of which is to criticise the common interpretation of Smith's gravitation metaphor. Smith uses it, not in a Newtonian sense to represent the attractive character of natural price, but rather in an Empedoclean or Aristotelian sense to illustrate the pattern of movement of market prices, a pattern for which natural price serves merely as a reference point.[28]

A second purpose is to present an alternative interpretation of Smith's natural price based on his understanding of nature. Smith asserts that the goals of nature are the self-preservation of individuals and the propagation of species, goals humans pursue with divided labour under bonds of mutual dependence, facilitated by exchange and hence prices. The natural price of a commodity is the price that supports nature's goals by providing for the maintenance of those who participate in production and supply in a manner that is just sufficient for these activities to continue indefinitely.[29]

The third purpose of this essay is to highlight the similarity between natural prices construed in this way and the prices of Piero Sraffa's *Production of Commodities by Means of Commodities: Prelude to a Critique of Economic Theory*. Although Sraffa moves beyond Smith in a number of ways, he begins from similar assumptions, taking as given a society with divided labour, addresses the same problem of mutual dependence among members of such a society, and reaches similar conclusions, invoking exchange and prices.

---

[27] Aspromourgos (2010) provides the most comprehensive discussion of Smith's use of nature and the meaning of natural price.

[28] Empedocles was the first to formulate the four elements theory, but Aristotle is responsible for its mature form.

[29] A natural price understood in this way may be the normal price, or it may not, but the term 'normal price' fails to capture the full meaning of Smith's 'natural price' because it does not reflect this purposive generative movement of Smith's nature. If a substitute for Smith's natural price is needed, 'reproduction price,' 'necessary price' or 'continuation price' would be superior to 'normal price' or 'ordinary price,' both of which for Smith could only apply to market prices.

This essay proceeds as follows. The first section examines the context in which Smith's gravitation metaphor appears in order to show that it was intended as an assertion about the movement of market prices rather than one about the meaning of natural price. Section Two explores the gravitation metaphor in detail to show that what Smith described is gravity in the ancient rather than the modern sense, implying that movement results from the inclination of market price rather than from any property of natural price. The third section focuses attention on Smith's understanding of nature, arguing that, according to Smith's Aristotelian usage, 'natural' refers to the reproduction of species, including the human species. Based on this discussion, Section Four presents an interpretation of the sense in which natural prices are said to be natural in Smith. Section Five turns to the prices of Sraffa's *Production of Commodities by Means of Commodities*, focusing on his discussion of the term natural price.

1. Gravitation in the Context of *Wealth of Nations* I.vii

Book I, Chapter VII of the *Wealth of Nations*, 'Of the Natural and Market Price of Commodities,' opens by postulating a society in which income is distributed among wages, profits and rents, in a manner with enough stability to justify the description of the rates of payments as 'ordinary': 'There is in every society or neighbourhood an ordinary or average rate both of wages and profit in every different employment of labour and stock' [and also rent] (WN I.vii.1). Smith defined these stable rates as the natural rates: 'These ordinary or average rates may be called the natural rates of wages, profit, and rent, at the time and place in which they commonly prevail' (WN I.vii.3).[30] Smith takes as given, that is, that the object of study is a stably ongoing society with a division of labour that distributes income according to ownership of land, labour and capital.

Smith defined 'natural price' on the basis of these postulated rates of income distribution: 'When the price of any commodity is neither more nor less than what is sufficient to pay the rent of the land, the wages of the labour, and the profits of the stock employed in raising, preparing, and bringing it to market, according to their natural rates,

---

[30] Although Smith called these prices natural he acknowledged that they are not purely natural in the sense of being necessary for physical reproduction, but have also a conventional element through the conventionality of wages. He argued that the natural rate of wages would tend to be that which is sufficient for the self-preservation of individuals, 'the lowest which is consistent with common humanity' (WN I.viii.16; also I.viii.28), but he made clear that this did not mean the minimum necessary for biological survival, distinguishing between a component of the wage that is absolutely necessary for physical survival, and a societal component which varied across different countries: 'By necessaries I understand, not only the commodities which are indispensably necessary for the support of life, but whatever the custom of the country renders it indecent for creditable people, even of the lowest order, to be without' (WN V.ii.k.3). Smith says that these 'may be called' the natural rates, even though he acknowledged that, strictly speaking, the natural rate of wages was not natural.

the commodity is then sold for what may be called its natural price' (I.vii.4).

Smith continued with two points about natural price, explaining first that the natural price is 'precisely ... what it is worth, or ... what [a commodity] really costs the person who brings it to market' (I.viii.5) and second that it 'is not always the lowest at which a dealer may sometimes sell his goods, it is the lowest at which he is likely to sell them for any considerable time' (I.vii.6). We will return to these points because they constitute Smith's explanation of natural price, but our concern here is with the gravitation mechanism, so it is only necessary to note that neither point Smith makes here about natural price involves any reference to any property of attraction or to market prices.

Only after having explained natural price does Smith introduce market price, defined as the 'actual price at which any commodity is commonly sold' (I.vii.7) and 'regulated by the proportion between the quantity which is actually brought to market, and the demand of those who are willing to pay the natural price of the commodity' (I.vii.8).

Smith next explained how this proportion expressing relative shortages and surpluses drives the movements of market prices, the former leading to increases in market prices, the latter to decreases. On this basis Smith explained how the 'quantity of every commodity brought to market naturally suits itself to the effectual demand,' a surplus leading to a fall in price and a reduction in the quantity brought, a shortage leading to an increase (I.vii.9-14).

It is at this point that Smith introduces the gravitation metaphor: 'The natural price, therefore, is, as it were, the central price, to which the prices of all commodities are continually gravitating. Different accidents may sometimes keep them suspended a good deal above it, and sometimes force them down even somewhat below it. But whatever may be the obstacles which hinder them from settling in this center of repose and continuance, they are constantly tending towards it' (I.vii.15).

The word 'therefore' directly links the claim to the previous discussion in which shortages and surpluses are eliminated through movements of prices, so the gravitation metaphor represents a summary of those movements. The natural price, described in terms only of its location as the 'central price,' serves as a reference point, as a metaphorical place, in terms of which Smith describes the movement of market prices. This involves no claim about properties of natural price, in particular, no claim that it has any power to attract market prices.

Smith goes on to discuss 'occasional and temporary fluctuations' in market prices and then systematic obstructions: 'particular accidents, sometimes natural causes, and sometimes particular regulations of police, may, in many commodities, keep up the market price, for a long time together, a good deal above the natural price' (I.vii.20).

Smith continues by setting deviations of market prices from natural prices aside: 'This is all that I think necessary to be observed at present concerning the deviations, whether occasional or permanent, of the market price of commodities from the natural price' (I.vii.32). He does this because both the random fluctuations as well as the more systematic obstructions make no contribution to the ongoing functioning of the economic system and are therefore logically independent of natural price. David Ricardo stated the same point more forcefully and directly:

> In the 7th chap. of the *Wealth of Nations*, all that concerns this question is most ably treated. Having fully acknowledged the temporary effects which, in particular employments of capital, may be produced on the prices of commodities, as well as on the wages of labour, and the profits of stock, by accidental causes, without influencing the general price of commodities, wages, or profits, since these effects are equally operative in all stages of society, *we will leave them entirely out of our consideration*, whilst we are treating of the laws which regulate natural prices, natural wages and natural profits, *effects totally independent of these accidental causes*. In speaking then of the exchangeable value of commodities, or the power of purchasing possessed by any one commodity, I mean always that power which it would possess, if not disturbed by any temporary or accidental cause, and which is its natural price. (1817, pp. 91-2; emphasis added)

Ricardo does not deny that deviations of market price from natural price occur, but rather claims that such deviations are independent of the determination of natural prices and based on conditions independent of the principles that regulate natural prices. Such deviations are, therefore, of no theoretical interest. In setting them aside, Smith and Ricardo treat market prices as equal to natural prices for their theoretical purposes.

Once deviations of market price from natural price are excluded, the process of adjustment Smith illustrated with the gravitation metaphor loses its *raison d'être* and is also excluded. The gravitation metaphor arises only in connection with these deviations of market price from natural price. The metaphor's significance and function disappear when these deviations are set aside.

The adjustment process that Smith likened to gravity, then, is separate from the determination of natural prices, describing the movements of market prices when they deviate from natural prices, movements that have no intrinsic theoretical interest. Along with the gravitation metaphor, it provides no clues as to the nature of natural price.

2. Empedoclean or Newtonian Gravitation?[31]

The idea of natural price as a 'normal price,' 'centre of gravity' or 'central attractor' involves interpreting Smith's gravity in a Newtonian sense as an attractive force between bodies: 'The power of attraction which, according to the [Newtonian] theory of gravity, each body possesses, is in proportion to the quantity of matter contained in that body' (*Astronomy* IV.75). Smith, however, was closely familiar with another understanding of gravity, the ancient view associated with the theory of the four elements, in its original form due to Empedocles.

Smith expressed his great admiration for Newton in his essay known as the 'History of Astronomy': 'The superior genius and sagacity of Sir Isaac Newton . . . made the most happy, and, we may now say, the greatest and most admirable improvement that was ever made in philosophy, when he discovered, that he could join together the movements of the Planets by so familiar a principle of connection, which completely removed all the difficulties the imagination had hitherto felt in attending to them' (*Astronomy* IV.67). But here we are concerned with a metaphor, so this is not a question of in which theory Smith had more confidence.

It has been noted by several writers that the sense in which Smith used gravity in explicating his famous metaphor is not quite Newtonian.[32] Referring to the gravitation metaphor, I. Bernard Cohen claims that Smith was Newtonian, but only imperfectly and incompletely, that what Smith 'took from Newton's physics was perfectly correct *up to a point*; it was merely incomplete. ... Often cited as an instance of Smith's alleged Newtonianism, this use of gravity is an illustration of imperfect replication.'

The problem, according to Cohen, is that 'Smith did not take account of one of the features of Newtonian gravitation,' namely, 'its property of acting mutually between all pairs of gravitating bodies, so that there is always an equal and opposite force.' According to Smith's metaphor market prices gravitate toward natural prices. If Smith were to replicate Newton's gravity correctly and completely, market prices would also exert a mutual gravitational pull on natural price: 'a complete homology with Newtonian physics would require that the natural price must also gravitate toward all other prices' (Cohen 1994, pp. 65-66).[33]

I argue that the sense of gravity in Smith's metaphor is not just imperfectly

---

[31] The question of Newton's influence on Smith is beyond the scope of this essay. See Redman (1993) and Montes (2003, 2006)

[32] Cf. Schliesser (2005, pp. 40-1).

[33] Sinha, commenting on this paper, suggests that the failure of Smith's natural prices and market prices to display Newtonian attraction is due the implicit assumption by Smith of constant returns to scale in each industry, but Sraffa (1926) has shown that the classical theory excludes the possibility of such a functional relationship between cost of production and quantity produced within an isolated industry.

Newtonian, but pre-modern, involving not a force of attraction drawing prices toward one another, but an inclination on the part of the market prices toward a central point of rest, a sense Smith described in his essay on *Ancient Physics*. According to the theory of the four elements, each element earth, water, air and fire, had 'a particular region allotted to it,' a 'place of rest, to which it naturally tended, by its motion, either up or down, in a straight line, and where, when it had arrived, it naturally ceased to move'. The levity of air and fire gave them a tendency to move outward away from the centre, while the 'natural motion' of water and earth, due to their gravity, 'was downwards, in a strait line to the center'. Once an element arrived in its allotted place, 'each of them tended to a state of eternal repose and inaction'.

Consider once more the relevant passage in this light: 'The natural price, therefore, is, as it were, the central price, to which the prices of all commodities are continually gravitating. Different accidents may sometimes keep them suspended a good deal above it, and sometimes force them down even somewhat below it. But whatever may be the obstacles which hinder them from settling in this center of repose and continuance, they are constantly tending towards it.'

There are three clear indications in the passage that this gravity is Empedoclean or Aristotelian rather than Newtonian. First, Smith's language indicates that the movement is the result of an inclination of the market prices, which are gravitating, tending to move as though they possessed gravity. There is no suggestion of Newtonian gravity as a mutually attractive force pulling two bodies together. Second, as with Empedocles, the direction those things with gravity tend to move is in a straight line toward a central point. Newtonian gravity pulls bodies in the direction of other bodies, lacking the notion of a centre or central point altogether. Third, the gravitation of market prices directs them toward achievement of a place 'of repose and continuance,' also an idea central to the ancient account of gravity but completely foreign to the Newtonian one.

The gravitation metaphor, then, reflects the movements of market prices but without contributing anything to the definition of natural price, just as the centre of the earth, according to the ancient theory, serves as the place of repose for those things with gravity without telling us anything about the centre of the earth in itself.

In order to understand Smith's natural price, then, it is necessary to turn away from the gravitation metaphor and to examine Smith's definition of natural price. It will be useful, however, to first consider what Smith understood in his use of nature and natural.

3. Adam Smith and the Purposes of Nature

Smith wrote repeatedly that the primary purposes of nature are the self-preservation of individuals and the propagation of species: 'Thus self–preservation, and the propagation of the species, are the great ends which Nature seems to have proposed in the formation of all animals' (*TMS* II.i.5.9, p. 77); 'In every part of the universe we observe means adjusted with the nicest artifice to the ends which they are intended to produce; and in the mechanism of a plant, or animal body, admire how every thing is contrived for advancing the two great purposes of nature, the support of the individual, and the propagation of the species' (*TMS* II.ii.3.5, p. 87). Since the self-preservation of individuals is a means to the propagation of the species, the former is subsumed under the latter and thus Smith also referred to the single purpose of nature as reproduction: '[Nature's] great purpose, the *continuance and propagation* of each species' (*ED* 23, p. 571).[34]

In this sense, nature, in pursuing its goal, is the cause of a certain systematic activity oriented toward continuation of the various kinds of natural bodies. This is a teleological sense in that the activity of which nature is the cause is directed at the achievement of goals or purposes.

This is not original, but strongly suggestive of Aristotle, who took the same view, joining the goals of self-preservation and reproduction as the primary intentions of nature and the primary focus of the activities of living beings: 'The life of animals, then, may be divided into two acts – procreation and feeding; for on these two acts all their interests and life concentrate' (*History of Animals* 589a 2-4). As Aristotle scholar Mariska Leunissen writes: 'The nutritive capacity is . . . the ultimate principle of life and the one capacity that is common to all living beings.' Aristotle defines it as the capacity for both reproducing and using food, which are the 'most natural functions' among living beings. (2010, p. 63). Similarly, philosopher Martha Nussbaum writes: 'This capacity – to maintain functional states through self-nutrition and to propagate them through reproduction – is the mark that set off the living from the lifeless' (1986, p. 76). In this sense Aristotle says that the nutritive capacity is the 'nature' of plants and animals: 'the nutritive soul . . . is also the generative soul, and this is the nature of every organism, existing in all animals and plants' (*Generation of Animals* 740b9-741a5).

Smith and Aristotle both believed that human beings were distinctive among animals for a number of reasons, but neither exempted humans from the overall goals of nature. According to Smith's *Lectures on Jurisprudence*, 'Food, cloaths, and lodging are all the wants of any animal whatever' (LJB.207, p. 487) including humanity, as he also identified these same things necessary for self-preservation as 'three great wants of mankind' (LJA vi.24, p. 340) and as 'our three humble necessities' (LJB.209, p. 488).

Like Aristotle, Smith suggested that satisfying these needs was a primary activity of human enterprise, although he recognised that while these are, in a sense, natural

---

[34] Smith also suggested that happiness was the purpose of human beings. The position, shared by Aristotle, does not contradict Smith's claims that nature's goals are self-preservation and reproduction, any more than it did Aristotle's. Self-preservation and reproduction are minimal conditions for all life, but different species have different and distinctive capacities beyond this.

necessities, they are not merely natural necessities: 'The whole industry of human life is employed not in procuring the supply of our three humble necessities, food, cloaths, and lodging, but in procuring the conveniences of it according to the nicety and [and] delicacey of our taste' (LJB.209, p. 488).

The pursuit of these necessities forms the basis for the activities of society more broadly: 'in a certain view of things all the arts, the sciences, law and government, wisdom, and even virtue itself tend all to this one thing, the providing meat, drink, rayment, and lodging for men' (LJA vi.20, p. 338). Money bears the same purpose: 'The intention of money as an instrument of commerce is to circulate goods necessary for men, and food, cloaths, and lodging' (LJA vi.127, p. 377).

In drawing this comparison between Smith's use of nature with respect to prices and Aristotle's understanding of nature, I should emphasise that I am not suggesting that Smith followed Aristotle's writings on economics, for example, on household management, exchange or chrematistics.[35]

Aristotle discussed at great length the nourishment and reproduction of non-human animals. Smith's discussion of human reproduction represents an extension of Aristotle's approach to the human species. This does not closely follow what Aristotle wrote about human economy, but it follows a direction that can be found in his other writings.

4. Natural Prices and the Purposes of Nature

Despite the similarity between humans and other animals as self-maintaining organisms, Smith emphasised the uniqueness of the human mode of meeting nature's purposes, of preserving one's self, which, unlike other animals, involves communication and cooperation. Smith asserts that adult non-human animals 'live intirely independent of others' unable to use the skills in combination with others: 'The swiftness of the greyhound, the strength and sagacity of the mastiff, and the docility of the sheep dog, as they do not occasion a division of work, no way ease the labour of the species. Each works for himself.'

Humans, on the other hand, possessed of language and the ability to cooperate, can work together by dividing labour and specialising. They are thus able to 'ease the labour of the species' or the group. Although born with few physical advantages compared with other animals, only humans are able to develop specialised skills in various fields of endeavour that are complementary to each other.

---

[35] On Aristotle's economic writings, see Crespo (2006, 2008a, 2008b, 2008c).

The division of labour, according to Smith, allows humans to be massively more productive than other animals, but it also creates a problem. Those who acquire and practice specialised skills are dependent on others for their subsistence (aside from use of what one produces one's self), so an advanced division of labour creates a situation of extreme mutual dependence. Thus, for Smith, as for Aristotle, people are inherently social, brought together by their need for each other: 'man ... can subsist only in society' (*TMS* II.ii.3.1).

Nature did not, according to Smith, leave it up to human beings to discover a means to manage this mutual dependence, but implanted within people an inclination to ('truck, barter' and) exchange which, Smith famously argues, is an effective means of gaining the cooperation of others under such circumstances and overcoming the problem of dependence:

> 'Man continually standing in need of the assistance of others, must fall upon some means to procure their help. This he does not merely by coaxing and courting; he does not expect it unless he can turn it to your advantage or make it appear to be so. Mere love is not sufficient for it, till he applies in some way to your self-love. A bargain does this in the easiest manner' (LJA vi.45, pp. 347-8; cf. WN I.ii.2).

Exchange therefore arises by nature and solves a problem created by nature in such a way as to allow for the realisation of nature's purpose, the survival of the human species. As the terms of exchange, prices are similarly connected to nature, playing a corresponding role in the accomplishment of nature's ends. From this perspective, the natural prices would be those that precisely fit nature's goals for humans, their survival, and this, I suggest, is what we find in the *Wealth of Nations*.

As noted above, Smith defined natural price in the *Wealth of Nations* as 'neither more nor less than what is sufficient to pay the rent of the land, the wages of the labour, and the profits of the stock employed in raising, preparing, and bringing it to market, according to their natural rates' (I.vii.4). Natural price equals the cost of production, but Smith's explanation shows that the significance of natural price extends beyond simply being the cost of production to contributing to the continuation of production.

Smith made two related points in explanation of his natural price. First, the natural price represents the value of a commodity from the perspective of the person who supplies the market and therefore includes profit: 'The commodity is then sold precisely for what it is worth, or for what it really costs the person who brings it to market'. Smith does not say explicitly why the perspective of the supplier should be privileged here, why the real cost to the person who supplies the commodity is what it is worth in a general sense, as opposed, for example, to what a commodity is worth according to the producer or the consumer, but the answer can be inferred from Smith's second explanatory comment: 'Though the price, therefore, which leaves him this profit, is not always the lowest at which a dealer may sometimes sell his goods, it is the lowest at which he is likely to sell them for any considerable time; at least where there is perfect liberty, or where he may change his trade as often as he pleases.'

The natural price is the lowest price that makes it possible for the supply of the commodity to continue 'for any considerable time.' Although this introduces a time element into the analysis, it is not the duration of periods of time that are at stake, but the possibility of ongoing continuation based on the revenue provided by the natural price: 'The natural price... is the lowest which can be taken, not upon every occasion, indeed, but for any considerable time together... the lowest which the sellers can commonly afford to take, and at the same time continue their business' (*WN* I.vii.27). This element of continuation ties natural price to the purposes of nature.

The perspective of the person supplying the commodity to the market is relevant, then, because that is the person whose role it is to continue supplying the market. Natural price is the price that is just sufficient to actuate the person with the capacity to allow business – production, supply and exchange – to continue in an ongoing, self-sustaining way.

We see the roots of this idea in Smith's *Lectures on Jurisprudence*, where the natural price is similarly tied to the division of labour and reproduction as the price that supports the continuation of business by incentivising the relevant specialised labour, as that price which 'is necessary to induce one to apply to a particular business,' sufficient not only to maintain the specialised labourer but also to compensate the costs of acquiring the specialised skills: 'Thus one would not become a hackneywriter unless he had a prospect of maintaining himself and recompensing the expense of education.'

While the maintenance of the labourer is crucial, the natural price must be sufficient not only to maintain the labourer, but to support continuing business activities, including the ongoing acquisition and practice of the specialised skills: 'Maintenance is the first thing necessary to be afforded by every business. But if this trade gives no more than bare maintenance this will not induce any one to enter into it. I perhaps having by some accident fallen into some strange out-of-the-way business, may by dint of application make a miserable lively hood of it, but if this be all, the trade will end in me.'[36]

Again, the natural price is the lowest price that will allow the business to continue indefinitely. It is not necessary that the business actually continue indefinitely or even for a long period of time in fact because for Smith natural price is the theoretical condition

---

[36] Smith likewise emphasised that natural wages must be sufficient not only for the self-preservation of the individual labourer, but also for the propagation of the species: 'They must even upon most occasions be somewhat more; otherwise it would be impossible for him to bring up a family, and the race of such workmen could not last beyond the first generation' (*Wealth of Nations* I.viii.15).

that must be satisfied for continuation regardless of whether the market price is greater, lower or equal to it.[37] If the condition is minimally satisfied, then the business is able to continue, if not, it will not.

Although natural price is equal to the cost of production, it is not simply the historical expense involved in the production that is at stake here, but the revenue that will be sufficient to continue the supply of commodities to the market, to keep commodities in motion, to continue the business. The revenue constituted by natural price is important not just because it is sufficient to pay the producer of the commodity that has been sold, but because it allows the process to go on. The natural price in both the *Lectures on Jurisprudence* and *Wealth of Nations* promotes the goals of nature, continuation of production, the self-maintenance of individuals and the reproduction of the system as a whole. The natural price, in both cases, is the price that fulfils the conditions necessary for ongoing production and hence allow for the survival of human beings and the propagation of the human species.

5. Natural Price and *Production of Commodities*

Piero Sraffa repeatedly called attention to the 'connection' between his book *Production of Commodities* and 'the theories of the old classical economists,' describing his own 'standpoint' as 'that of the old classical economists from Adam Smith to Ricardo' (1960: v) and suggesting that the classical term 'natural price' would be a suitable label for the prices of his own models.

The similarities between Smith's natural price and Sraffa's prices can be seen in Sraffa's discussion of price concepts and terms, but it will be necessary to trace Sraffa's path to get to that discussion.

As with Adam Smith's discussion of natural price, Sraffa began *Production of Commodities* by postulating a society that continues to exist stably over time because it produces enough output, with a division of labour supported by exchange among mutually dependent producers: 'Let us consider an extremely simple society which produces just enough to maintain itself. Commodities are produced by separate

---

[37] In later lectures, Smith added compensation for risk to the list of expenses that natural price must cover if ongoing production is to be sustained: 'A man then has the natural price of his labour when it is sufficient to maintain him during the time of labour, to defray the expense of education, and to compensate the risk of not living long enough and of not succeeding in the business. When a man has this, there is sufficient encouragement to the labourer and the commodity will be cultivated in proportion to the demand' (LJB.227, pp. 495-6).

industries and are exchanged for one another at a market held after the harvest'
(1960, p. 3).[38]

Sraffa begins then, as does Smith's discussion of natural price, by taking a living, producing economic society with division of labour as given and asking how this society continues to survive as a stable unified entity. On the basis of just a few simple assumptions – that commodities are produced in single product industries with no surplus and exchanged with a single price for each commodity – Sraffa demonstrates that the problem can, as Smith suggested, be solved through exchange: 'There is a unique set of exchange-values which if adopted by the market restores the original distribution of the products and makes it possible for the process to be repeated; such values spring directly from the methods of production' (1960, p. 3).

Sraffa's claim that the values 'spring directly from the methods of production' has often been taken to mean that prices are determined solely by technology, for example, 'relative prices depend on the conditions of production' (Woods 1990, p. 16, 31), because each equation represents a production process. This formulation, however, conceals the role of the condition of reproduction, which does not appear as a variable in any of the equations, but is the condition for the solution of the equations. The requirement of reproduction drives the solution of the equations in a manner analogous to the way that the equilibrium condition drives the solution of supply and demand equations. The magnitudes of the prices will depend on technology, but they are prices with a purpose, that is, to facilitate reproduction.

As in Smith, the division of labour and the dependence that it creates plays a crucial role throughout *Production of Commodities* – reproduction requires exchange among distinct industries as each requires inputs from others. This contrasts sharply with Marshall's assumption that the forces that determine prices can be isolated in supply and demand functions peculiar to a given industry.

Sraffa's next model, of production with a surplus and a corresponding uniform rate of profit, follows the same principles. Sraffa then introduced the well-known distinction between basic and nonbasics, between those commodities that play a role in the determination of the system of prices and those that do not, on the basis of whether they enter, directly or indirectly, into the production of every other commodity. The prices of basic commodities play a role in the determination of the system of prices as a whole while the prices of non-basics do not:

---

[38] Sraffa does not address money, which plays no role in *Production of Commodities*, but it is not explicitly excluded either. Money might be used to facilitate exchange within the market held after the harvest, but Sraffa did not specify any of the institutional details through which that exchange is carried out, except in vague terms a market after the harvest.

'These products have no part in the determination of the system. Their role is purely passive. If an invention were to reduce by half the quantity of each of the means of production which are required to produce a unit of a [non-basic] commodity of this type, the commodity itself would be halved in price, but there would be no further consequences; the price-relations of the other products and the rate of profits would remain unaffected. But if such a change occurred in the production of a commodity of the opposite type [basic], which does enter the means of production, all prices would be affected and the rate of profits would be changed' (1960, p. 8).

Sraffa's discussion of natural price immediately follows the introduction of the distinction between basic and non-basic commodities. Up to that point, Sraffa described the exchange ratios of his system as prices and values, but then suggested that it 'might be thought more appropriate' that 'costs of production' be used instead. The question concerns the conceptual relationship between prices and costs of production and the meaning of the terms. It might be suggested that the mathematical structure is more important than what the variables are called. Mathematically, prices equal costs of production, the values depending on the equations and not at all on their names. But this was not the view of Sraffa for whom the point was terminological and theoretical rather than mathematical.

Sraffa claimed that the term 'cost of production' is an appropriate description of the prices of nonbasic commodities because they simply reflect their costs of production and nothing beyond: 'their exchange ratio is merely a reflection of what must be paid for the means of production, labour and profits in order to produce them – there is no mutual dependence'.

The situation of a basic commodity, however, is different in that its price is not only equal to what was paid to produce it, but also has 'another aspect to be considered' in its role in the reproduction of the system as a whole: its 'exchange ratio depends as much on the use that is made of it in the production of other basic commodities as on the extent to which those commodities enter its own production' (1960, p. 9).

For this reason, Sraffa argues, to label the prices of his model 'costs of production' would be misleading except with respect to nonbasics. A broader term is needed, that is, one that captures the fact that the price of a basic commodity is equal to its costs of production, but also captures the fact that it is determined by its role in the reproduction and continuation of the overall system: 'a less one-sided description than cost of production therefore seems to be required'.

For the sake of brevity, Sraffa does not use Smith's natural price, but according to Sraffa, natural price does capture this aspect of the prices of basics: 'Such classical terms as "necessary price", "natural price", or "price of production" would meet the case' (1960, p. 9).

In Sraffa's view, that is, 'natural price' as used by Smith does not share the one-sidedness of 'cost of production' and captures the other aspect, 'the use that is made of' a commodity, its participation in the reproduction of the system as a whole.

Although Sraffa develops the point much further than Smith does, this notion of basicness as something equal to costs of production but moving beyond to include participation in the determination of the system as a whole parallels what I have argued about Smith's definition and explanation of natural price – that it is equal to the costs of production, but also that it is important for reasons that do not merely look backward at production but forward to use of the revenue to continue business in a self-maintaining way.

In this way Sraffa develops a price concept close to Smith's concept of natural price, without any mention of market prices or the adjustment process Smith compared to gravitation, consistent with Ricardo's claim that deviations of market prices from natural prices are of no theoretical interest. In excluding market prices, then, Sraffa followed the examples set by Smith and Ricardo.

Conclusion

Sraffa and Smith begin from the same place and ask the same question. Both begin with a given economic system characterised by a division of labour that exists and continues to exist through time. That such a society exists is evidence that it maintains and reproduces itself, in the sense that any thing that actually exists, as Aristotle pointed out, must be in a constant state of continuing its existence by maintaining itself and reproducing itself through time – otherwise it would have ceased to exist. The question to be directed at any such existent, according to Aristotle's approach, is how, in what manner, it manages to carry out this activity of ongoing existence. The answer to this question corresponds to the nature and content of animal life.

Both Smith and Sraffa answer that exchange plays the key role with the price system providing the conditions for continuing reproduction and the ongoing survival of the human species. Those prices, that are just sufficient to provide for ongoing production, supply and exchange, may, therefore, be called natural prices because they support the purposes of nature. These prices, independent of the deviation of market prices from natural price and the gravitation-like adjustment process, are equal to costs of production, but involve something more than simply cost of production. They contribute to the feeding, reproduction, and continuation of humanity.

Acknowledgements

I gratefully acknowledge comments on the paper made in the *Economic Thought* Open Peer Discussion Forum by Leonidas Montes, Maria Elton and Ajit Sinha.

References

Aristotle (1942) *Aristotle: Generation of Animals*. Translated by A. L. Peck (Cambridge, MA: Harvard University Press).

Aristotle (1878) *Aristotle's History of animals. In ten books*. Translated by R. Cresswell (London: G. Bell).

Aspromourgos, T. (2009) *The science of wealth: Adam Smith and the framing of political economy* (London: Routledge).

Cohen, I. B. (1994) 'Newton and the social sciences, with special reference to economics, or, the case of the missing paradigm,' in Philip Mirowski, *Natural Images in Economic Thought: 'Markets Read in Tooth and Claw'* (Cambridge: Cambridge University Press), pp. 55-90.

Crespo, R. F. (2006) 'The Ontology of the "Economic": an Aristotelian Analysis', *Cambridge Journal of Economics*, 30 (5) pp. 767-781.

Crespo, R. F. (2008a) 'Aristotle's Science of Economics', in Samuel Gregg and Ian Harper (eds.), *Christian Morality and Market Economies: Theological and Philosophical Perspectives* (Edward Elgar), pp. 13-24.

Crespo, R. F. (2008b) '"The 'Economic" According to Aristotle: Ethical, Political and Epistemological Implications', *Foundations of Science*, 13 (3-4) pp. 281-294.

Crespo, R. F. (2008c) 'Aristotle', in Irene van Staveren and Jan Peil (eds.), *Elgar Handbook of Economics and Ethics* (Cheltenham and Northampton), pp. 14-20.

Eatwell, J. and Milgate M. (1999) 'Some deficiencies in Walrasian intertemporal general equilibrium,' in Gary Mongiovi and Fabio Petri. *Value, Distribution and Capital* (Routledge), pp. 82-93

Garegnani, P. (1976/2003) 'On a Change in the Notion of Equilibrium in Recent Work on Value and Distribution: A Comment on Samuelson.' In *The Legacy of Piero Sraffa*. Volume 2, edited by Heinz D. Kurz and Neri Salvadori, pp. 451-471.

Harcourt, G.C. and Kriesler, P. (2012) Introduction (To *Handbook of Post-Keynesian Economics* (Oxford University Press: USA)). UNSW Australian School of Business Research Paper No. 2012-33.

Kurz, H. and Salvadori, N. (1998) *Understanding 'Classical' Economics: Studies in long-period theory* (London: Routledge).

Leunissen, M. (2010) *Explanation and Teleology in Aristotle's Science of Nature* (Cambridge: Cambridge University Press).

Marshall, A. and Marshall, M. P. (1879) *The Economics of Industry* (London: Macmillan).

Montes, L. (2003) 'Smith and Newton: some methodological issues concerning general economic equilibrium theory', *Cambridge Journal of Economics*, 27 (5) pp. 723-47.

Montes, L. (2006) 'On Smith's Newtonianism and general equilibrium theory,' in L. Montes and E. Schliesser eds. *New Voices on Adam Smith* (Routledge), pp. 247-70.

Nussbaum, M. C. (1986) *Aristotle's De Motu Animalium.* (Princeton: Princeton University Press).

Redman, D.A. (1993) 'Adam Smith and Isaac Newton,' *Scottish Journal of Political Economy*, 40 (2) pp. 210-230.

Ricardo, D. (1966) *The Works and Correspondence of David Ricardo*, Volume I *On the Principles of Political Economy and Taxation.* Edited by Piero Sraffa (Cambridge University Press).

Schliesser, E. (2005) 'Some Principles of Adam Smith's Newtonian Methods in the Wealth of Nations: In Memoriam: I. Bernard Cohen.' In *Research in the History of Economic Thought and Methodology: A Research Annual*, edited by Warren J. Samuels, Jeff E. Biddle, and Ross B. Emmett, 33-74, vol. 23-A.

Smith, A. (1759/1976) *The Theory of Moral Sentiments* (Oxford: Clarendon Press). (TMS)

Smith, A. (1762/1978) *Lectures on Jurisprudence* (Oxford: Clarendon Press). (LJ)

Smith, A. (1776/1976) *An Inquiry into the Nature and Causes of the Wealth of Nations.* (Oxford: Clarendon Press). (WN)

Smith, A. (1795/1980) On the Principles that Lead and Direct Philosophical Enquiries, illustrated by the History of Astronomy (HA); by the History of the Ancient Physics (AP); by the History of the Ancient Logics and Metaphysics. In *Essays on Philosophical Subjects* (Oxford: Oxford University Press).

Sraffa, P. (1926) 'The Laws of Returns under Competitive Conditions', *Economic Journal*, 36 (44) pp. 535-550.

Sraffa, P. (1960) *Production of Commodities by Means of Commodities; Prelude to a Critique of Economic Theory* (Cambridge University Press).

Woods, J. E. (1990) *The Production of Commodities: An Introduction to Sraffa* (Atlantic Highlands, NJ: Humanities Press International).

SUGGESTED CITATION:

Andrews, D. (2014) 'Adam Smith's Natural Prices, the Gravitation Metaphor, and the Purposes of Nature'. *Economic Thought*, 3.1, pp. 42-55.
http://www.worldeconomicsassociation.org/files/journals/economicthought/WEA-ET-3-1-Andrews.pdf

Economics as a Science, Economics as a Vocation: A Weberian Examination of Robert Heilbroner's Philosophy of Economics

Daniyal Khan, Graduate student at the Department of Economics, The New School for Social Research, New York, USA
daniyalk@gmail.com

Abstract

In an attempt to re-envision economics, the paper analyses Robert Heilbroner's philosophy of economics through the lens of Max Weber's philosophy of science. Specifically, Heilbroner's position on vision, ideology and value-freedom is examined by contextualising it within a framework of Weberian science. Doing so leads to a better understanding of Heilbroner's seemingly contradictory statements about ideology as well as a re-interpretation of his position on the place of value-freedom (or a lack thereof) in economics. This inquiry also leads to a demonstration of (1) the relevance of Weber's work on methodology of science to contemporary issues in economics, and (2) the identification of a major shortcoming in Heilbroner's work. Overall, this leads to a clarification and reconstruction of Heilbroner's vision of economics as a science and as a vocation, which is seen to be a self-reflexive, reflective and dynamic process.

Keywords: Heilbroner, Weber, economics, methodology, vision, ideology

1. Introduction

1.1 Robert Heilbroner, an Economist: The Task at Hand, Context, and Scope

Given the state of economics (Blaug, 1998, 2001; Kay, 2011) there is a need to re-imagine and re-envision the discipline. This paper is an exploratory exercise in such a re-imagination which takes Robert Heilbroner's work as a starting point. Two factors make Heilbroner's work a suitable choice. His work presents a unique perspective on economics from within the discipline, taking a historically aware and self-critical approach, all the while keeping a keen eye on questions of methodology. Much of his work is comprised of commentary on, and critique of, the state of economics (Heilbroner, 1994a,

1995; Heilbroner and Milberg, 1997) and by virtue of the fact that many of the problems with economics that he pointed out continue to persist, his work continues to be relevant. What is important is that Heilbroner's criticisms and assessments are not those of an outsider, but of an insider – he served as vice-president of the American Economic Association in 1984. His work provides a reliable and trustworthy picture of economics from the point of view of a person who skilfully navigated the space between economic orthodoxy and the margins of the discipline.

Secondly, his work has been engaged with and recognised by his contemporaries. The commentary on his work points out his contributions and shows the breadth and depth of his thought. For example, Milberg (2004, p. 236) points to the curious nature of Heilbroner's work as both historically conscious and 'forward-looking' and Dimand (2004, p. 389) has noted that 'Heilbroner was also a pioneer in appreciating Polanyi's importance.' Furthermore, Forstater (2004, p. 1) notes that Heilbroner was 'aware of environmental-economic challenges from remarkably early on' and Canterbery (2001, p. 333) places Heilbroner within 'a uniquely American tradition of social criticism.' Gilkey (1975) analyses Heilbroner's 'vision of history' from the perspective of the respective places of science and religion in times to come, as well as their relationship with each other. In exploring these less-discussed aspects of Heilbroner's work, Gilkey has pointed towards the bigger issues being raised by Heilbroner with regards to modern society.

Hence, if we are to refer to the work of an economist to help us re-imagine economics, an examination of Heilbroner's work seems to be a good place to start. We take a seeming contradiction in his views on ideology as a point of departure into this examination. It appears that he does not always take a negative view of ideology. In fact, he has argued for the legitimacy and necessity of ideology. Related to these issues, is his position that not only is value-freedom in economics impossible, but also, that it is undesirable. This evidence from Heilbroner's work stands in stark contrast with that part of his writing in which he categorically denounces ideology as a negative phenomenon. The question arises whether these two seemingly contradictory views can be held at once by the same person or not, and if so, then how. The emphasis placed by Heilbroner on vision and his position on value-freedom in economics are both related to his position on ideology and must also be examined further. What is required is an examination of Heilbroner's philosophy of economics.

There is one important qualification to be added with regards to the scope of this paper. Heilbroner discusses ideology on many different levels, and in many different contexts. Thus, it is important to ask: ideology of what or whom? As we will see, his view of ideology, by virtue of the possibility of defining it in many different ways, is difficult to deal with. This makes it important to specify the level of ideology or the context in which it is being discussed. While this is not *the* point being argued in the paper, it is certainly one of the larger issues which the paper points towards: the possibility of a plurality of understandings of ideology which are context-dependent.

The qualification I would add to my general argument is as follows. Let us envision an economist. He (or she) lives and works within a scientific community. That scientific community, in its varying material conditions, may find within itself people belonging to different classes. These classes live within a larger social setup which we can identify as capitalism, and we can see that members of a larger scientific community can have links with other groups within capitalism; industry, for example, or finance. In this small exercise, we have moved from the individual economist to capitalism in general. Ideology permeates all these different layers or levels of social life in different ways. With the particular purpose of trying to better understand the internal dynamics and process of economics as a social science in Heilbroner's view, my paper merely discusses his view of ideology in the very specific context of how the individual economist thinks and works within the scientific community.

Heilbroner of course thinks that social scientists' points of view are related to their position in society, as will be seen later in the paper. Those parts of his work where he does discuss this point would help us make the link between 1) ideology of economists as individuals, of economists as a group, and as members of a scientific community, and 2) ideology of capital (1985, p. 107). My paper however, merely addresses the former. This in no way implies that the latter is not important in terms of how we understand the former. In fact, the influence of the latter on the former may well be indispensable in understanding not only the economics discipline as it is today but also how it has come to be the way it is today. These themes are, however, beyond the scope of the current study and may be explored in the future.

A comment about the larger context of Heilbroner's ideas is warranted. His take on ideology is interesting for two main reasons. Firstly, ideology as a broad theme remains a neglected area in the mainstream of the discipline. For example, for those looking for an introduction to the theoretical and empirical relationships between economics and ideology, Oxford's *A Dictionary of Economics* (Black et al., 2009) offers nothing. Secondly, Dobb (1973, p. 3) points to the significance of Joseph Schumpeter's contribution to this issue, in which the latter employed the concept of 'vision' in relation to ideology and economics. Heilbroner's position on ideology and vision, directly and openly Schumpeterian in its intellectual lineage, thus deserves attention in any contemporary discussion of the relationship between economics and ideology. Furthermore, the relegation of values to the separate field of welfare economics and the consequent strengthening of the positivist commitment to value-freedom within the mainstream of the discipline (Putnam and Walsh, 2012, p. 3) stands diametrically opposed to Heilbroner's position on value-freedom, as we will see. Against the background of the division between positive and normative economics, and the position that economics must aspire to value-freedom for it to qualify as a science (Block, 1975, p. 38) Heilbroner's position seems radical and deserves a closer look.

1.2 Max Weber: An Intellectual Affinity and Relevance

This examination of Heilbroner's understanding of vision, ideology and value-freedom will be conducted using a Weberian interpretative lens. To put together this lens, the paper will rely on (1) Max Weber's essay 'Science as a Vocation' and on (2) secondary literature on Weber's view of science, its purposes, characteristics and relation with the principle of value-freedom. By extracting some relevant insights from this literature (which comprises the work of Karl Lowith and Basit Bilal Koshul), and by complementing it with evidence from Heilbroner's own work, the paper hopes to provide a relational reading of Heilbroner's work. This should lead to a clarification of Heilbroner's position.

Why Weber? Weber's stature in the social sciences and his extensive work on the methodology of the social sciences is widely recognised and thus justifies using his work as a touchstone and interpretative lens. The possibility of a further refining and clarification of Heilbroner's thought when viewed from the lens of Weber's methodology of (social) science(s) is an exciting prospect which, if realised, can contribute to the secondary literature on Heilbroner's ideas. Besides this, it could also potentially show the continued relevance of Weber's work to contemporary problems in economics, his past contributions to economics already established (Engerman, 2000).

Still, why Weber? Why not take the methodological work of some other social scientist? There is, I believe, a fundamental and strong intellectual affinity between Weber and Heilbroner which has been overlooked by the literature on Heilbroner's work, and which justifies using Weber's work as the analytical lens. Demonstrating, as I believe, that this affinity is the result of a direct influence of Weberian ideas on Heilbroner is a research project in itself, and is as such beyond the scope of this paper. However, to indicate the basic evidence which has led to this belief, I would point to two key ideas in Heilbroner's thought which seem to express what are at core Weberian ideas.

The first point is that Heilbroner's characterisation of vision (1990, p. 1112) reflects the central Weberian insight that certain values, taken as starting points of worldviews, ultimately stand opposed to each other and their 'validity' cannot be proven or disproven in an absolute sense. In Heilbroner's context, this would mean differing –

even opposing – visions taken as starting points of different kinds of analytical paths. The second point is that Heilbroner's view of economics as possessing an instrumental function (Heilbroner and Milberg, 1997, p. 125) reflects Weber's own instrumental view of science as presented in 'Science as a Vocation.' The evidence presented in sections 2 and 3 should corroborate these points further.

An important question about the relevance and viability of the Weberian framework for examining Heilbroner's work remains. Considering that ideology is not an explicitly discussed theme in 'Science as a Vocation,' (and presumably in the Weberian corpus at large, considering that an entry on ideology is not to be found in *The Max Weber Dictionary: Key Words and Central Concepts* (Swedberg, 2005)), to what extent is the classroom context of 'Science as a Vocation' relevant and useful in helping us understand Heilbroner's ideas about ideology? I would point out here that Weber's vision of science as an instrument of self-understanding is fundamentally akin to Heilbroner's vision of economics as capitalism's instrument of self-understanding (Heilbroner, 1994a, p. 8). The classroom is one of the many forums on which this self-understanding is developed, challenged, and transmitted from generation to generation. The scientific community at large is another such forum, only bigger. The classroom, while not a big part of Heilbroner's discussion of ideology, vision and value-freedom, is relevant because of the central place it occupies within the economics profession as the location of transmission of economic doctrine, including ideology.

The paper is organised as follows. Section 2 reviews Heilbroner's position on vision, ideology and value-freedom and show the relations among the three. Section 3 reviews Weber's view of science as presented in 'Science as a Vocation.' It also reviews the interpretation of Weberian science provided by Lowith and Koshul and the insights from their work relevant to the issue at hand. Specifically, it shows Weberian science to be a dynamic and continuous process rather than a static and mechanical process. Sections 4 and 5 analyse Heilbroner's philosophy of economics through a Weberian lens. That is, by contextualising vision, ideology and value-freedom within a framework of Weberian science, they reconstruct Heilbroner's vision of economics as a science and as a vocation, and discuss the insights gained from this analysis. Section 6 concludes the paper.

2. Heilbroner on Vision, Ideology, Value-freedom, and the Purpose of Economic Analysis

The term vision is understood by Heilbroner as follows:

'the political hopes and fears, social stereotypes, and value judgments – all unarticulated, as we have said – that infuse all social thought, not through their illegal entry into an otherwise pristine realm, but as psychological, perhaps existential, necessities. ... "vision" sets the stage and peoples the cast for all social inquiry' (Heilbroner and Milberg, 1997, p. 4).

Furthermore, 'our individual moral values, [and] our social angles of perception' (Heilbroner and Milberg, 1997, p. 4) are also part of our vision. Hence, vision precedes analysis and sets the analytical agenda. Heilbroner (1988, p. 198) holds that visions are not true or false – they cannot be proven or disproven historically. He concedes that 'while not denying their wishful character, I see visions as free of the exaggerations and inconsistencies that we commonly associate in a pejorative sense with ideologies' (1990, p. 1109). Despite this, he insists that vision is to be 'celebrated' because of its 'immense constructive power' (1988, pp. 198-199). The purpose visions serve is that they 'structure the social reality to which economics, like other forms of social inquiry, addresses its attention' (1990, p. 1112). This structuring and constructing of reality is the reason that vision is necessary for analysis (1988, p. 198).

The problem with understanding Heilbroner's view of ideology arises because of what can be called an almost schizophrenic view of ideology. Firstly, ideological elements are a part of vision (Heilbroner, 1993, p. 93). For Heilbroner, ideology is (1) 'biased discourse' (Heilbroner and Milberg, 1997, p. 114) (2) 'claims of universality' (Heilbroner and Milberg, 1997, p. 114) (3) 'unknowing deception of the self' (Heilbroner, 1995, p. 26) – all having negative connotations. He also claims that ideology is 'irremovable,' (1988, p. 193) and differentiates between 'blatant' and concealed ideologies (1988, pp. 189-190). On the other hand, he claims that ideology is legitimate and necessary for analysis inasmuch as ideology is part of vision and vision is itself necessary for analysis (1993, p. 94; 1994b, pp. 325-329).

Heilbroner's opposition to value-freedom is largely linked to his view of the role of the economist and his/her social context. Firstly, Heilbroner believes that the distinction between the economist and the economic statistician is that the former, in his attempt to explain social phenomena, infuses meaning into his data. For Heilbroner (1973, p. 131), this infusion of meaning is an act which makes economics value-laden. This infusion of meaning is directly related to visions. Heilbroner (1990, p. 1112) sees 'visions as expressions of the inescapable need to infuse "meaning" – to discover a comprehensible framework – in the world.' Secondly, the economist's work is closely tied to his own social context. Economics cannot be value-free because the economist cannot remove himself from his own social context:

> 'Indeed, at the risk of making an assertion that verges on a confession, I would venture the statement that every social scientist approaches his task with a wish, conscious or unconscious, to demonstrate the workability or unworkability of the social order he is investigating. ...
>
> Moreover, this extreme vulnerability to value judgments is not a sign of deficiency in the social investigator. On the contrary, he belongs to a certain order, has a place in it, benefits or loses from it, and sees his future bound up with its success of failure. In the face of this inescapable existential fact, an attitude of total "impartiality" to the universe of social events is psychologically unnatural, and more likely than not leads to a position of moral hypocrisy' (Heilbroner, 1973, p. 139).

A last feature of Heilbroner's philosophy of economics which is worth reviewing is his proposal for serious consideration of the possibility of a political economics (Heilbroner, 1970). Political economics would entail telling the economist that the social and political goal 'x' is desired. The economist would then make clear as to what means could be employed to achieve that end, and what they would entail. The economist is not in any privileged position more than anyone else in deciding which socio-political ends are desirable. Determination of socio-political ends will be the political project/enterprise. What this means is an 'instrumental reorientation of economics' (Heilbroner, 1970, p. 18).

3. Key Features of Weber's Philosophy of Science

Having seen Heilbroner's position on vision, ideology and value-freedom, we now turn to Weber's view of science. We will first review a handful of relevant characteristics of a Weberian view of science (though these are not the only ones): that it offers clarity as a goal, that it is based on presuppositions and values which are not provable by its own methods, and that despite an affirmation of these values at its base, it ought to be value-free by becoming aware of these presuppositions and by accounting for them. As this discussion proceeds, Weber's view of science will be seen to be a dynamic, continuous and creative process rather than a static and mechanical one.

In 'Science as a Vocation,' Weber offers us the three contributions of science. The one most pertinent to the issue at hand is the third one: science helps us 'gain clarity'

(Weber, 1969, p. 151).[39] The scientist sets out for others a choice map of sorts. Rather than saying that you ought to aim for this end, he instead tells us that if you wish to obtain this end, you have at your disposal such and such different paths. Each path brings with it such and such implications. That is, '*if* you take such and such a stand, then, according to scientific experience, you have to use such and such a *means* in order to carry out your conviction practically' (Weber, 1969, p. 151). In doing so, the scientist can give a person '*an account of* the *ultimate meaning of his own conduct*' (Weber, 1969, p. 151).

However, science itself must first begin somewhere, and it begins with certain presuppositions (Weber, 1969, p. 143). Besides presupposing the validity of its methods, science also presumes that the things it wishes to know are 'worth being known' (Weber, 1969, p. 143). According to Weber:

> 'In this, obviously, are contained all our problems. For this presupposition cannot be proved by scientific means. It can only be *interpreted* with reference to its ultimate meaning, which we must reject or accept according to our ultimate position towards life' (Weber, 1969, p. 143).

Furthermore, each specific science will have its own specific presuppositions. As Koshul notes:

> 'all sciences studying empirical reality, ... are based on suprarational factors such as presuppositions, evaluative ideas—and ultimately on a suprarational affirmation of the validity of these presuppositions and evaluative ideas' (Koshul, 2005, p. 47).

Moreover, 'Weber asserts that cultural values play a critical role in bringing order to the chaotic form of an observed phenomenon that presents itself to the observer' (Koshul, 2005, p. 47).

Weber's principle of value-freedom is well known and need not be discussed in much detail. In as much as science lends its assent to its presuppositions as an act of faith, does it not become value-laden when it should be value-free? How then, is it possible to have value-free science? This point is clarified in a passage by Koshul worth

---

[39] The first contribution is that it 'contributes to the technology of controlling life by calculating external objects as well as man's activities.' The second is that it gives us 'methods of thinking, the tools and the training for thought' (Weber, 1969, p. 150).

quoting at length. Koshul's own reading of Weber depends on Karl Lowith's interpretation of Weber's essay 'Science as a Vocation':

> 'Weber seems to be saying that, while science is based on certain subjective factors and value judgments, it is at the same time free of certain subjective factors and value judgments. This apparent contradiction in Weber's thought is clarified by Lowith in these words.
>
> "What Max Weber's call for a value-*free* science sought none the less to demonstrate was that, in spite of science's emancipation, its 'facts' were underpinned by specific preconceived value-judgments of a moral and semi-religious type, some of which even approximated to fundamental principles. Science was to become free, in the sense that its value-judgments were to become decisive, logically consistent and self-reflexive, rather than remaining concealed, both to others and to science itself, under the cloak of 'scientific knowledge.' Weber's call for the value-freedom of scientific judgement does not represent a regression to pure scientificity; on the contrary, he is seeking to bring those extra-scientific criteria of judgment into the scientific equation. ..." (Lowith, 1989, p. 146)
>
> For Weber, the value-free character of science is not related to the fact that it is free of subjective factors and value judgments of a "moral and semi-religious type." Science is value-free in the sense that its "moral and semi-religious" dimension has become "decisive, logically consistent and self-reflexive, rather than remaining concealed." Science becomes science only when its extra-scientific dimension is explicitly recognized, accounted for, and made clear. As long as the extra-scientific, semireligious dimension of science remains concealed from the view of the scientist, science falls short of being science' (Koshul, 2005, p. 47).

In the passage by Lowith quoted by Koshul, Lowith goes on to write:

> 'what Weber demands is not an eradication of the "value-ideas" which provide science with its criteria, but the objectification of these ideas as a pre-condition for the adoption of what seemed to him a possible critical distance from them' (Lowith, 1989, p. 146).

Thus, science first fully commits itself to its value-ideas and is only then able to become 'value-free' by creating a distance between itself and its values. Koshul interprets this relationship between the fundamental values which underpin science and value-freedom in another manner consistent with Lowith's interpretation. In his study of Weber, Koshul (2005, p. 144) goes on to show that 'for Weber, the praxis of science must precede any fruitful reflection on the methods of science.' As reflection on the methods succeeds praxis, the scientist 'should not shrink from the possibility of having to revise the "logical forms" of the "enterprise" – even if this revision means the reformulation of the very "nature" of the work' (Koshul, 2005, p. 144). That is, before science can revisit its fundamental values which determine the logical forms of science, it must first commit itself to these values and *then* examine its fundamental commitments. In doing so, it may have to 'tweak' its fundamental evaluative ideas, thereby changing the logical forms and nature of its praxis from then onwards.

From the evidence presented in this discussion, we can view Weberian science to be a dynamic and creative process which can roughly be described in three stages. Note that understanding Weber's view of science in such a manner runs the risk of presenting it again as a static and linear process. What is intended, however, is only to use this depiction of Weberian science as a heuristic device which will allow us to analyse Heilbroner's views in the next section. The three stages are as follows:

1. Affirmation of presuppositions and evaluative ideas (a) without which science cannot begin, and (b) which give order to observed phenomena,
2. Scientific praxis as a means to gaining clarity about the best means to achieve a given/desired end,
3. Reflection on methodology, revisiting values affirmed at Stage 1 and revealing the previously concealed values-judgments; revision of logical forms and nature of science if the need be.

It is Stage 3 which is crucial to science's dynamism. When the basic evaluative ideas and methodology are revisited, some of them may be found wanting and others may be found to be as relevant and necessary as before. Thus, depending on the degree to which one will revise one's basic evaluative ideas and methodology, one will revise the nature of scientific praxis. As was said before, the division of science into a three-stage process serves only as a heuristic device which risks looking at the three stages as being mutually exclusive. In fact, each of the three stages can be seen to interact with the other two in a unique way. Every particular case of Stage 3 can also be seen as a 'new' Stage 1, and vice versa. Furthermore, Stage 3 itself is not mutually exclusive with Stage 2. Once the very first affirmation of the value of science is made and scientific praxis has begun, each particular case of reflection on methodology will be a part of scientific praxis, rather than lying outside its domain. In as much as every Stage 3 is a new Stage 1, Stage 1 also then becomes part of scientific praxis. It is these dynamics of science which make it self-reflexive.

4. Heilbroner's Philosophy of Economics through a Weberian Lens

We now begin to place vision, ideology and value-judgments in the Weberian framework of science outlined above. First and foremost, all of vision, including its ideological aspects, can be placed under the heading of Stage 1. For economic (scientific) analysis to begin, there must be the affirmation, even if unconscious or unarticulated as Heilbroner says, of certain presuppositions and evaluative ideas: 'political hopes and fears, social stereotypes and value-judgments' as well as 'our individual moral values.' That is, as Heilbroner says, there *must* be vision. Furthermore, this vision cannot be proved using the methods of economic science.

The second stage is scientific praxis. Economic analysis is part of the scientific praxis of economics. The scientific praxis of the economist requires him/her to help us gain clarity about the most suitable means to achieve any desired end. A more specific part of the praxis of an economist specified by Heilbroner is crucial to understanding Heilbroner's views contextualised within the three-stage process of Weberian science. This element of praxis is the writing of a reflective journal:

> 'Like the natural scientist, the economist (or for that matter, any social scientist) is expected to keep his journal, recording as best as he can his starting points, his successive steps, his final conclusions. He records, with all the honesty and fidelity of which he is capable, not only his data and his processes of reasoning, but his initial commitments, hopes, and disappointments' (Heilbroner, 1973, p. 143).

This process of journal writing – part of the economist's praxis – directly and smoothly transitions into Stage 3, for it requires, in part, the explicit articulation of the economist's vision which had initially been unarticulated. Now we see that at Stage 3, vision – including the economist's values and ideological leanings – must come under scrutiny and may need to be first articulated, and then revised if need be. Thus vision, ideology and values placed in the context of the three-stage Weberian framework outlined above make economics as a science and a vocation to appear as follows:

1. Affirmation of vision, ideology, values and evaluative ideas (a) without which economics cannot begin, and (b) which structure and construct reality,
2. Economic praxis (analysis and journal writing) as a means to gaining clarity about the best means to achieve a given/desired end,
3. Reflection on vision and ideology, revisiting vision and ideology affirmed at Stage 1 and articulating the previously unarticulated visionary elements; revision of logical forms and nature of economics if the need be.

5. Discussion

By contextualising values, ideology, vision in this Weberian view of science, a number of insights emerge. Firstly, Heilbroner's position that vision is unarticulated must be interpreted to mean that vision is only unarticulated *at first*: that is, at the very first instance of Stage 1. Self-consciousness and laying bare of the economists' basic presuppositions and evaluative ideas which is to happen at Stage 3 requires articulation. For example, Heilbroner himself articulated (or made explicit) the vision of the worldly philosophers in his work, and others like Milberg, Gilkey and Canterbery have articulated (or made explicit) Heilbroner's vision. Left unarticulated, the ideological elements within vision cannot be identified, let alone scrutinised. Furthermore, even the non-ideological elements of vision may lose their legitimacy if vision is left unarticulated because without articulation, these parts of vision can also not be made explicit for 'painful self-scrutiny' (Heilbroner, 1973, p. 142). From this perspective, the vision and ideology distinction becomes possibly irrelevant. If vision as a whole is to be subjected to 'public examination' (Heilbroner, 1973, p. 143), so will the ideological elements within it. If, however, all of vision is left unexamined, so will the ideological elements in it.

Secondly, we see that ideology as unknowing self-deception *is* legitimate, in-so-far as it allows for the beginning of scientific praxis (Stage 1). However, once scientific praxis begins, the economist will be obliged as part of his practice to try and articulate his vision (including its ideological aspects) in his journal (Stage 2) and then return to it to reflect on it and in the process identify the ideological elements within it and to change them (Stage 3). In doing so, he will be able to make his vision and its ideological elements, in Lowith's words, part of the scientific equation. He will then be able to account for them in his analysis. Ideology can also be understood as what Lowith calls the objectification of value-ideas which then allows for a critical distance from them (i.e. value-freedom).

Thirdly, as Heilbroner says, ideologies (and thus also visions) are alterable (1988, p. 193). Heilbroner himself takes up this task in his work, of proposing a new vision. Thus, visions must be consciously edited. As the socio-political context of the economist's inquiry changes, say over his lifetime,[40] vision may also change unconsciously and new ideological elements may enter it accordingly. Heilbroner himself admits that there is never a shortage of ideologies (1993, p. 91). Thus at Stage 3, 'science goes about its task, exposing itself to informed criticism at every stage of its inquiry, engaging in painful self-scrutiny with regard to its premises, experiments, reasoning, conclusions' (Heilbroner, 1973, p. 142). That is, (economic) science as this three-stage process must be continuous and dynamic – it must be self-reflexive.

Fourthly, as was discussed earlier, Heilbroner does not wish for economics to be a value-free science and does not think it to be possible for it to be so. However, it appears that Heilbroner himself has laid the ground for a value-free economics as a possible eventuality in the specifically Weberian understanding of value-freedom reviewed earlier. Heilbroner's insistence on constructing more relevant visions and scrutinising ideological visions – and thus the value-judgments, presuppositions and evaluative ideas embodied in those visions – lends itself to this thesis. Despite claiming to 'urge the abandonment of the idea of a "value-free" economics' (Heilbroner, 1973, p. 143) Heilbroner in fact *did* allow for the possibility of a Weberian value-freedom, albeit unintentionally, in the conclusion of his essay 'Economics as a "Value-Free" Science':

> 'Rather, I want economics to make a virtue of necessity, exposing for all
> the world to see the indispensable and fructifying value-grounds from
> which it begins its inquiries so that these inquiries may be fully exposed
> to—and not falsely shielded from—the public examination that is the true
> strength of science' (Heilbroner, 1973, p. 143).

This desire effectively embodies Lowith's interpretation of Weberian value-freedom.[41]

---

[40] Or even over generations, in which case, we can think of science as a social enterprise in place of an individual scientist.

[41] Anghel Rugina (1998, pp. 821-824) is of the opinion that Heilbroner is unable to offer a solution to the problem of value-freedom. However, Rugina's conclusion is based on a completely different methodological approach, including an interpretation of Weber which, in my understanding, is different from that of Koshul and Lowith, through whose work I have accessed Weber's thought.

All of this seriously undermines Heilbroner's claim that ideology is 'irremovable' (1988, p. 193). If ideology is irremovable, then the question arises as to what is the point of self-scrutiny and public examination of one's value-commitments. It also raises the question of why this self-scrutiny is painful if not because of the realisation of the self-deceptive nature of ideology. Having admitted the legitimacy of ideology at the very first instance of Stage 1, room must be made now for the self-conscious eradication of ideology and re-construction of vision at every successive Stage 3. Indeed, that is exactly what Heilbroner has attempted to do in much of his own work.

An attempt ought to be made to explain why it is that Heilbroner describes self-scrutiny as being painful. This will be attempted, again, from a Weberian perspective arising from a reading of Weber's 'Science as a Vocation.' The ideological elements in vision which are synonymous with unknowing self-deception can be understood to cover up what Weber (1969, p. 147) calls 'inconvenient facts.' The role of the scientist *qua* teacher is to bring about in his students an awareness of 'facts that are inconvenient for their party opinions' (Weber, 1969, p. 147). In doing so, he/she successfully weeds out the ideological elements in a person's vision. This self-scrutiny with the aid of the scientist is painful exactly because it makes us aware of our deception of ourselves. This pain can also be viewed from another perspective. Koshul (2005, p. 119) states that 'for Weber, an investigator takes up the investigation of a particular subject because he/she seeks to better understand the factors that are challenging or undermining a particular value-commitment that he/she has.' If such is the case and if we come to realise the validity of the factors which undermine a particular value to which we are committed, we become aware of the ideological and self-deceptive nature of that particular value; thus the pain.

Furthermore, Weber's position, that the ideas and values involved at what has been called Stage 1 are actually required to make sense of reality and to allow us to analyse it, can be seen as theoretical capital which could have been employed by Heilbroner to support his 'valorization of vision' (1993, p. 93). This has three important implications. Firstly, it shows that Weber's work on methodology of the social sciences still remains relevant to economics. Secondly, it shows a neglect of Weber's methodological capital on Heilbroner's part. Surely, referring back to one of the major methodologists of the social sciences to find support for a major idea in his work would have been fruitful. Thirdly, it also gives Heilbroner's position legitimacy from a Weberian perspective.

6. Conclusion

Analysing Heilbroner's position on vision, ideology and value-freedom in economics through the lens of a Weberian philosophy of science allows us to see a number of things. Firstly, it allows us to clarify and better understand Heilbroner's philosophy of economics as a science and as a vocation. We see the different contexts of the conflicting understandings of ideology and the possibility of its removal, the dynamic and self-reflexive nature of economics as a science and as a vocation, the need for reflection as part of an economist's vocation (and implicitly, the need for the cultural richness which such self-critical reflection requires), a possible re-understanding of Heilbroner's position on value-freedom, and potential explanations of the reasons for the painful nature of self-scrutiny.

Secondly, it shows us the relevance of Weber's methodological capital to contemporary issues in economics. The presence of ideology in economics is a major concern for Heilbroner; the fact that 'the actual and very positive goal of his [i.e. Weber's] epistemological essays is *the radical dismantling of "illusions"*' (Lowith, 1993, p. 148) makes Weber's work a potential resource which can be employed to dismantle illusions within economics. Thirdly, it allows us to identify a shortcoming in Heilbroner's work: an absence of direct reference to Weber's methodological capital, which could have allowed him to expound his thesis for the valorisation of vision and condemnation of ideology with greater force and clarity.

To summarise, the paper has argued that **IF** we accept that:

(1)   Lowith and Koshul's interpretation of Weber's philosophy of (social) science and value-freedom forms one valid interpretative lens among many, and

(2)   Heilbroner is a fair representative of the discipline of economics and that his work is still relevant to contemporary issues in the methodology of economics,

and we then use the interpretative lens mentioned in (1) to analyse Heilbroner's ideas about ideology, vision and the methodology/philosophy of economics in general, **THEN** it appears that:

(A)   Heilbroner's philosophy of economics as a science and as a vocation can be clarified and refined, and allows us to see economics as a dynamic and self-reflexive science, and

(B)   Weber's work has a continuing relevance to contemporary issues in the methodology of economics, which suggests that Weber's work perhaps needs to be re-visited more thoroughly for new insights.

It appears that an absence of an explicit reference to ideology in 'Science as a Vocation' and the classroom context of Weber's essay do not impede on the ability of the Weberian framework to help us better understand Heilbroner's thought. This is because of the crucial point that the problems the two of them are exploring are very much of the same nature. The paper's arguments could be made stronger by devoting a complete research project to clearly establishing the link between Weber and Heilbroner, especially with regards to the influence of the former on the latter. Moreover, Weber's ideas about methodology have only been employed in their least potent form, without reference to his other methodological writings. These lines of inquiry, should they be pursued, should provide interesting insights about facets of Heilbroner's work which have yet been left unexplored.

As economics develops, evolves and hopefully moves forward, we can assess the work of a number of economists through a number of different interpretative lenses, which would result in a large variety of perspectives and lines of inquiry. Each such combination will yield (or not) its own lessons and problems. By analysing Heilbroner's philosophy of economics through a particular kind of Weberian lens, we come to a very specific understanding of his work, which in turn gives us a very particular way to approach economics – a particular way to envision and imagine economics. Whether or not this particular approach is worth theoretically exploring – even practically attempting – is an issue I invite the readers to debate and discuss.

Acknowledgements

I am grateful to the following people for their respective contributions: Professor Basit Bilal Koshul, whose guidance was central in helping me develop the ideas expressed in this paper; Atiyab Sultan, whose comments and feedback during the infancy of this project provided invaluable impetus; Anders Fremstad and others present at The New School – University of Massachusetts Amherst Economics Graduate Student Workshop 2013, for their comments; Professor Robert McMaster and Professor Mark Peacock, whose comments on the open peer discussion forum provided constructive criticism which forced me to clarify my ideas further. The responsibility for all mistakes and shortcomings in the paper falls squarely on my shoulders alone.

References

Black, J., Hashimzade, N., and Myles, G. (eds.) (2009) *A Dictionary of Economics* (Oxford: Oxford University Press).

Blaug, M. (1998) Disturbing Currents in Modern Economics. *Challenge*, 41 (3), pp. 11-34 [online]. Available from: http://www.jstor.org/stable/40721829 [Accessed 12th July 2012].

Blaug, M. (2001) No History of Ideas, Please, We're Economists. *The Journal of Economic Perspectives*, 15 (1), pp. 145-164 [online]. Available from: http://www.jstor.org/stable/2696545 [Accessed 4th May 2012].

Block, W. (1975) Value Freedom in Economics. *The American Economist*, 19 (1), pp. 38-41 [online]. Available from: http://www.jstor.org/stable/25602990 [Accessed 15th January 2014].

Canterbery, R. E. (2001) *A Brief History of Economics: Artful Approaches To The Dismal Science* (Singapore: World Scientific Publishing Co).

Dimand, R. W. (2004) Heilbroner and Polanyi: A Shared Vision. *Social Research*, 71 (2), pp. 385-398 [online]. Available from: http://www.jstor.org/stable/40971702 [Accessed 16th January 2014].

Dobb, M. (1973) *Theories of Value and Distribution Since Adam Smith: Ideology and Economic Theory* (Cambridge: Cambridge University Press).

Engerman, S. L. (2000) Max Weber as economist and economic historian. In: Turner, Stephen. (ed.) *The Cambridge Companion to Weber* (Cambridge: Cambridge University Press), pp. 256-271.

Forstater, M. (2004) Visions and Scenarios: Heilbroner's Worldly Philosophy, Lowe's Political Economics, and the Methodology of Ecological Economics. *The Levy Economics Institute Working Paper Collection, Working Paper no. 413*, pp. 1-23 [online]. Available from: http://www.levyinstitute.org/pubs/wp413.pdf [Accessed 6th March 2012].

Gilkey, L. (1975) Robert L. Heilbroner's Vision of History. *Zygon*, 10 (3), pp. 215-33.

Heilbroner, R. L. (1970) On the Possibility of a Political Economics. *Journal of Economic Issues*, 4 (4), pp. 1-22 [online]. Available from: http://www.jstor.org/stable/4224050 [Accessed 16th January 2012].

Heilbroner, R. L. (1973) Economics as a "Value-Free" Science. *Social Research*, 40 (1), pp. 129-143 [online]. Available from: http://socsci.wikispaces.com/file/view/Heilbroner+-+Economics+as+Value-free+Science.pdf [Accessed 13th January 2012].

Heilbroner, R. L. (1985) *The Nature and Logic of Capitalism* (New York: W. W. Norton & Company).

Heilbroner, R. L. (1988) *Behind the Veil of Economics: Essays in the Worldly Philosophy* (New York: W. W. Norton and Company, Inc).

Heilbroner, R. (1990) Analysis and Vision in the History of Modern Economic Thought. *Journal of Economic Literature*, 28 (3), pp. 1097-1114 [online]. Available from: http://www.jstor.org/stable/2727102 [Accessed 9th December 2011].

Heilbroner, R. (1993) Was Schumpeter Right After All?. *The Journal of Economic Perspectives*, 7 (3), pp. 87-96 [online]. Available from: http://www.jstor.org/stable/2138444 [Accessed 3rd January 2012].

Heilbroner, R. (1994a) Taking the Measure of Economics. *Challenge*, 37 (6), pp. 4-8 [online]. Available from: http://www.jstor.org/stable/40722761 [Accessed 2nd January 2012].

Heilbroner, R. (1994b) Vision in Economic Thought: Remarks upon Receipt of the Veblen-Commons Award. *Journal of Economic Issues*, 28 (2), pp. 325-329 [online]. Available from: http://www.jstor.org/stable/4226819 [Accessed 4th May 2012].

Heilbroner, R. (1995) The Nature of Economics. *Challenge*, 38 (1), pp. 22-26 [online]. Available from: http://www.jstor.org/stable/40722719 [Accessed 9th December 2011].

Heilbroner, R. and Milberg, W. (1997) *The Crisis of Vision in Modern Economic Thought* (Cambridge: Cambridge University Press).

Kay, J. (2011) John Kay: The Map Is Not the Territory: An Essay on the State of Economics. *INET Blog* [online]. Posted 4 October, 2011.
Available from: http://ineteconomics.org/blog/inet/john-kay-map-not-territory-essay-state-economics [Accessed 28th December 2011].

Koshul, B. B. (2005) *The Postmodern Significance of Max Weber's Legacy: Disenchanting Disenchantment* (New York: Palgrave Macmillan).

Lowith, K. (1989) Max Weber's Position on Science. In: Lassman, P., Velody, I., and Martins, H. (eds.) *Max Weber's "Science as a Vocation"* (London: Unwin Hyman), pp. 138-156.

Lowith, K.(1993) *Max Weber and Karl Marx* (London: Routledge).

Milberg, W. (2004) The Robert Heilbroner Problem. *Social Research*, 71 (2), pp. 235-250.

Putnam, H. and Walsh, V. (2012) Introduction. In: Putnam, H. and Walsh, V. (eds.) *The End of Value-Free Economics* (Abingdon: Routledge), pp. 1-5.

Rugina, A. N. (1998) The problem of values and value-judgments in science and a positive solution: Max Weber and Ludwig Wittgenstein revisited. *International Journal of Social Economics*, 25 (5), pp. 805-854 [online]. Available from:

http://www.emeraldinsight.com/journals.htm?issn=0306-
8293&volume=25&issue=5&articleid=1502486&show=pdf [Accessed 13th January 2012].

Swedberg, R. (ed.) (2005) *The Max Weber Dictionary: Key Words and Central Concepts* (Stanford: Stanford University Press).

Weber, M. (1969) Science as a Vocation. In: Gerth, H. H. and Mills, C. Wright. (trans. and eds.) *From Max Weber* (New York: Oxford University Press), pp. 129-156.

SUGGESTED CITATION:

Khan, D. (2014) 'Economics as a Science, Economics as a Vocation: A Weberian Examination of Robert Heilbroner's Philosophy of Economics'. *Economic Thought*, 3.1, pp. 56-69.
http://www.worldeconomicsassociation.org/files/journals/economicthought/WEA-ET-3-1-Khan.pdf